My Great Grandmother's Lost, Banned, Burned Book

A Miraculous Find

Maureen Polasek Viaclovsky

My Great-Grandmother's Lost, Banned, Burned Book
A Miraculous Find

Inquires should be addressed to:
Maureen Viaclovsky
2106 Airline Drive
Friendswood, Texas 77456

E-mail: maureen.viaclovsky@gmail.com

ISBN13: 9781453793824

First Edition: September 2010

The information in this book is true and complete to the best of our knowledge. All recommendations are made without guarantee on the part of the author or publisher. The author and publisher disclaim any liability in connection with the use of this information.

Printed in the United States of America

My Great-Grandmother
MARIE DUJKA JEZ

Author of
KATECHISMUS MANŽELŮ
(A Married Couples' Catechism)

About the Photos on the Book Cover

The family members depicted in the photos on the front cover of this book are (clockwise, starting at the top, center photo): Marie Jez and family; Marie Jez; Frank Jez, Sr.; Marie Jez in her car; Josef & Veronica Surovcak Jez's daughters - left to right: Clara Jez Hubenak, Bessie Jez Polasek, Mary Jez Ernstes, Vera Jez Hereford; Josef and Veronica Surovcak Jez; Bessie Ann Jez Polasek; the original book cover of Marie Dujka Jez's book.

Ordering Information

Additional copies of this publication for self or for gifts to others (e.g., to children and other family descendants), may be ordered from www.createspace.com/3480560 or Amazon.com. Search on Amazon.com or other websites, such as Google.com, for the author's name or the book title: *My Great-Grandmother's Lost, Banned, Burned Book: A Miraculous Find.*

Contact the author if you are unable to locate copies of this book or would like to offer additional information.
E-mail: maureen.viaclovsky@gmail.com

For genealogy buffs, surnames mentioned in this book include the following: **Adamik, Alvarez, Barta, Beca, Becica, Bercak, Bergeron, Bolf, Boone, Brenk, Brod, Caves, Cerny (spelled "Cerna" in Czech), Cervenka, Chalupa, Cho, Cico, Connelly, Cook, Dujka, Dusek, Duyka, Ernstes, Faktor, Foltyn, Flowers, Gardner, Grigar, Hadjik, Haedge, Harrison, Hereford, Hubenak, Janik, Jez, Jones, Jurek, Kapavik, Kay, Klecka, Korenek, Kostalnik, Krchnak, Krecicek, Kubricht, Kulcak, Kulhanek, Lastovica, Listak, Lubojacky, Macik, Malek, Martisek, Mican, Mieth, Mikes, Mize, Mlcak, Nezhoda, Orsak, Pavlicek, Pavlovsky, Peacock, Pechal, Peters, Polasek, Provazek, Pyka, Raska, Reuss, Rickaway, Rousseau, Saha, Schauerte, Schiller, Schneider, Sebestiana, Smith, Sodolak, Somer, Sommer, Sowa, Surovcek, Svoboda, Thomas, Toman, Tomanec, Tuma, Tyl, Vaclavic, Vaclavick, Vargus, Viaclovsky, Vrazel, Ward, Whiclep, Yoshinaga.**

PREFACE

Marie Dujka Jez authored a book in the Czech language entitled *Katechismus Manželů (A Married Couple's Catechism),* which was originally copyrighted in 1926. The publication reflects Marie's progressive 1900s-era philosophy and advice for women and their spouses about the purpose of life, marriage, birth control, procreation, parenting, and natural home remedies.[1]

The original translation of the book into English was completed by Bessie Ann Jez Polasek, one of Marie's granddaughters, in 1984. This book includes (a) contributions by the author, Maureen Polasek Viaclovsky (Bessie's daughter); (b) a short story introduction by Marie's granddaughter, Bessie Ann Jez Polasek; (c) two introductory sections from the original 1926 edition that were authored by Marie's friend, M.F.K. Cerny[2]; (d) the English translation of Marie's book; and (e) photographs.

Throughout this book, the author's notes were inserted either for clarification or to provide additional information to the reader. The author's contributions are italicized, bracketed or footnoted.

---

[1] *For genealogy buffs, surnames mentioned in this book include the following: Adamik, Alvarez, Barta, Beca, Becica, Bercak, Bergeron, Bolf, Boone, Brenk, Brod, Caves, Cerny (spelled "Cerna" in Czech), Cervenka, Chalupa, Cho, Cico, Connelly, Cook, Dujka, Dusek, Duyka, Ernstes, Faktor, Foltyn, Flowers, Gardner, Grigar, Hadjik, Haedge, Harrison, Hereford, Hubenak, Janik, Jez, Jones, Jurek, Kapavik, Kay, Klecka, Korenek, Kostalnik, Krchnak, Krecicek, Kubricht, Kulcak, Kulhanek, Lastovica, Listak, Lubojacky, Macik, Malek, Martisek, Mican, Mieth, Mikes, Mize, Mlcak, Nezhoda, Orsak, Pavlicek, Pavlovsky, Peacock, Pechal, Peters, Polasek, Provazek, Pyka, Raska, Reuss, Rickaway, Rousseau, Saha, Schauerte, Schiller, Schneider, Sebestiana, Smith, Sodolak, Somer, Sommer, Sowa, Surovcek, Svoboda, Thomas, Toman, Tomanec, Tuma, Tyl, Vaclavic, Vaclavick, Vargus, Viaclovsky, Vrazel, Ward, Whiclep, Yoshinaga.*

[2] *M.F.K. (Marie) Cerny authored the introductory sections to Marie's original book and assisted Marie Jez to publish the book. A letter written by Aurelia Janik Cerny presents a convincing argument regarding the probable identity of Marie Cerny. Please refer to the letter at the end of this book. (Incidentally, the Czech version of Marie Cerny's surname was spelled "Cerna" in the original book.)*

The reader is urged to read the **footnotes** carefully for additional knowledge and enjoyment.

Much of the information was informally gathered by the author from the recollections of family and friends, few written records were available, and thus it is recognized that this book may have some unintentional historical errors, omissions, and inconsistencies.

In addition, the translation and editing of this work may have resulted in inadvertent modification of original author's intent. The author apologizes for these possibilities, and cannot be held liable for such.

Background Information,
Acknowledgements and Dedication

Translation of the book was a lengthy and laborious process conscientiously performed by Bessie Ann Jez Polasek, one of Marie's granddaughters. Bessie Ann utilized a typewriter to type the book in Czech, and then translated it into English in longhand, preserving the original Czech text wording as accurately as possible. Her work commenced on December 17, 1979, and was completed around June 29, 1984.

Bessie Ann was the daughter of Marie Jez's oldest son, Josef Jan Jez. Bessie Ann accessed a Czechoslovakian language dictionary for help and occasionally consulted her spouse, Charles Paul Polasek, who was also Czech-literate, and other Czech-language-knowledgeable family and peers for assistance.

Bessie's daughter, Maureen Polasek Viaclovsky, initially worked on editing and word processing the manuscript from December 5, 1985, through approximately August 13, 1986. Maureen performed additional revisions and editing in January of 1987, in July of 1993, and her work on this book commenced on September 6, 2003, and was completed on August 21, 2010.

Sincere thanks go to all relatives who contributed to the contents of this book, especially the following: Bessie's sister Vera Jez Hereford (Vera contributed several recollections) and Vera's daughter, Jo Ann Hereford (Jo Ann worked on scanning many of the original photos for this publication and their identification); Bessie's sister Mary Jez Ernstes (Mary contributed several recollections and photos) and Mary's daughters, Therese Ernstes Schneider and Casmary Ernstes Kay (Therese and Casmary helped gather photos); Bessie's sister Clara Jez Hubenak (Clara provided family history recollections, original photos, editing guidance, and encouragement to the author); Bessie's daughter Jane Veronica Polasek Connelly and her husband, Charles (Chuck) Connelly, who provided several photos and genealogy data.

Very special thanks also go to Sister Anna Marie Vrazel (Sister Anna Marie's mother was Marie Pavlicek Vrazel, the daughter of Marie's child, Olga Jez Pavlicek) and also to Susan Duyka Harrison (Susan's great grandfather was Marie's brother, John Duyka (Dujka)[3]. Sister Anna Marie and Susan contributed important genealogy data, and Susan organized a successful Dujka/Duyka family reunion on July 20, 2002, which provided the author with additional motivation to persevere with her work on this book. Willie and Irene Raska, of Wallis, Texas, contributed Willie's recollections about Marie's car and a photo. Additional acknowledgments are located elsewhere throughout the book.

Thankful appreciation must also go to Marie F. K. Cerny ("M.F.K. Cerny") (spelled "Cerna" in Czech and in Marie Jez's book). The two introductory sections to Marie Jez's book were penned by Marie Cerny, and reveal that she was similarly intelligent, reflective, and befriended and supported Marie Jez and was instrumental in facilitating the original Czech publication of Marie's book.

Information contributed by Aurelia Janik Cerny, presents a convincing argument regarding the probable identity of Marie Cerny as Marie Sommer (spelled "Somer" on the tombstone) Cerny, the wife of Vaclav Cerny. Please refer to Aurelia's letter of explanation, dated 11/8/2005, at the end of this book. **Many thanks to Aurelia Janik Cerny for this contribution.**

Finally, it is important to acknowledge that this book would not have become a reality without the invaluable guidance and skill of Gloria Hander Lyons, an experienced author whose many delightful publications can be found at www.BlueSagePress.com. A bouquet of thanks is offered to Gloria, and another to Marilyn Zapata, a dear friend and fellow author who led Maureen to Gloria.

---

[3] *The spelling of "Dujka" was altered to "Duyka." Perhaps Marie's brother John or his children mistook the "j" for a "y".*

Very special appreciation goes to Bessie Ann Jez Polasek, who lost a bout with breast cancer on January 1, 1990. An English edition of Marie's book would not have been forthcoming without Bessie's determination and dedication.

This book is lovingly and gratefully dedicated to Bessie Ann Jez Polasek by her daughter, Maureen Polasek Viaclovsky

Bessie Ann Jez Polasek

My beloved grandmother, Veronica Surovcak Jez,
who set this book in motion by forbidding my mother
to read my great-grandmother's book.

About my Great-Grandmother, Marie Jez

Author's note: The description that follows is based on the author's personal impressions formulated during the reading of Marie's book, during genealogy research, and during informal conversations with relatives and elders regarding their recollections, some of which were based on hearsay.

Most of the genealogy information in this section, "About My Great-Grandmother, Marie Jez" was taken from documents formulated and/or gathered by Sister Anna Marie Vrazel and Susan Duyka Harrison, and also from the combined recollections of Bessie Jez Polasek and her sisters Clara Jez Hubenak, Mary Jez Ernstes and Vera Jez Hereford.

Additional data was collected by Bessie's youngest daughter, Jane Veronica Polasek Connelly. For genealogy purposes, it should be noted that the spelling of "Dujka" was later altered to "Duyka," perhaps by Marie's brother John or his children (perhaps the "j" was mistaken for a "y"). [4]

Marie Dujka Jez's book provides a fascinating "peek" into the opinions, thoughts, philosophy and advice of Marie (Mariana) Dujka Jez, a woman who lived during the late 1800s and early 1900s era. She was born on September 8, 1859[5], in Slusovice, Moravia (present day "Czech Republic"), in the county of Vizavoice.

---

[4] *Sister Anna Marie is a granddaughter of Frank & Marie Jez's oldest daughter (Olga Jez Pavlicek). Sister Anna Marie's parents were Marie Pavlicek & Donat Vrazel. Susan Duyka Harrison is a great granddaughter of Marie's brother John (Dujka) Duyka. Susan's paternal grandfather was Joe Duyka, & her father's name is Ray Duyka.*
[5] *Sister Anna Marie Vrazel recalled that her grandmother (Olga Jez Pavlicek) told her mother (Marie Pavlicek Vrazel) that Marie rejoiced because her September 8th birthday fell on the Catholic holy day "Feast of the Blessed Mother."*

Marie's parents were Frantisek Dujka and Katerina Becica Dujka. Frantisek was born March 20, 1814, in Lipa, a village near Slusovice (house No. 28). He died March 25, 1879. Katerina was born on March 9, 1830, in Trnava (house No. 68). She came over to the United States from Austria at the age of 56 on December 7, 1886.

She came through Galveston with her daughters Karolina and Eleonora. Some research indicated that Katerina traveled to Texas in a covered wagon.[6] The 1900 Texas census lists Katerina as living with Eleonora, but she is not listed on the 1910 census as living with Eleonora. Katerina was reported to have been buried somewhere under a tree in West Poplar, near Bryan, Texas.[7]

Frantisek and Katerina's children were Frances, Marie, John (DOB December 2, 1860), Karolina (DOB July 8, 1863), Anna (DOB March 3, 1866), and Eleonora (DOB December 15, 1874). Frances became a nun (Sister Sebestiana) and never immigrated to the United States. Karolina never married. She lived with her sister, Marie, until her death, and is buried near Marie in the Catholic cemetery in Wallis, Texas.

John married Katherine Kulcak and they settled in Texarkana, Texas. Anna married John Vaclavick, Sr., and they lived in the Blessing and El Campo, Texas, areas.[8] Eleonora married John

---

[6] *This was suggested in research was gathered by Jane Veronica Polasek Connelly, Bessie's youngest daughter. 1920 census data for Austin County, Texas, town of Wallis, which was gathered by Mrs. Clinton Duyka (Mary Beca Duyka, whose husband is the son of Marie's brother, John Duyka), indicated that Marie came to America in 1884, about 2 – 3 years before her mother and sisters Karolina and Eleonora came & 3 years after her brother John Duyka. The 1920 census also states she became a citizen in 1910.*

[7] *This research was also gathered by Jane Veronica Polasek Connelly with additional 1920 census data provided by Mary Beca Duyka. Additional information regarding where Katerina lived and is buried was discovered in 2010 & is located on the page with her picture, later in this volume.*

[8] *According to information sent to the author by Elizabeth Pavlovsky Brod (whose mother, Josephine Brenk Pavlovsky, was born to John Duyka's daughter, Mary Duyka Brenk), the Vaclavicks lived in Bay City. Elizabeth's information came from family history notes collected by Elizabeth's maternal*

Nezhoda and although they lived in Texas initially, they moved to Oregon after their children were born. They are buried in St. Luke's cemetery in Hubbard, Oregon, in the Nezhoda family plot.

Marie attended grade school in Slusovice and was educated in Catholic convents in Europe. Initially, Marie attended a convent called "Austrie Hungaria Notra Dome Pozoney Convent," (this is believed to be the convent her sister, Frances, was in). Subsequently, Marie attended another convent called "Viden" or perhaps "Venia."

Marie left the religious order and immigrated to Texas. It is unknown whether she met her husband, Frank Jez, in Europe, or in Ellinger, Texas, where they are believed to have initially settled before moving to Wallis, Texas, sometime during the mid-1890's.

Frank was born October 6th, 1860, in "Karlorbovice" or "Kozlovice" county, in the city of Hrozenkov in the Moravia area (spelling of the city and county may be incorrect here). It is not known whether he was born in "Old" Hrozenkov or "New" Hrozenkov.[9]

A marriage certificate was prepared for Frank and Marie's descendants in 1969 by a priest at St. John's Church in Fayetteville, Texas. It records their marriage date as November 17th, 1886, when Marie was 27 and Frank was 26. Other data suggests they may have married several years earlier.[10]

---

uncle, Victor Brenk, who obtained it from Christine Duyka Mican, the daughter of John Duyka's son Joe.

[9] *In the Czech Republic, different sections of cities are designated as "old" & "new."*

[10] *Susan Harrison sent the author some data indicating that Mary Beca Duyka (Mary Beca Duyka is married to Clinton Duyka, the son of Anton Duyka, John Duyka's eldest son) unearthed some documents with the following information regarding settlement in Wallis, Texas: "On July 14, 1894, John & Catherine Kulcak Dujka legalized the purchase of about 90 acres of land one mile south of the town of Wallis, Austin County, Texas, sold to them by NP Ward for $1,027.40. John's sister, Mary Dujka Jez & her husband Frank also bought a parcel of land from NP Ward on the exact same day." This suggests that Frank and Marie were married earlier than 1886, and that John Dujka & his sister*

4

Marie and Frank had at least eight children. Two were females who died at very young ages. [11] They are buried at Hostyn (near Ellinger), Texas. Their surviving children were Josef ("Joe"), Frank Jr., Fridolin ("Fred")[12], Norbert, Olga, and Annie. Josef married Veronica Surovcak, Frank Jr. married Mary Hadjik, Fridolin married Frances Surovcak, Norbert married Louise Pavlicek, Olga married Vaclav Pavlicek, and Annie married Frank Lastovica. [13] Frank Jez Sr. died June 30, 1911, at age 50. In 1921, Marie moved into the city limits of Wallis.

The content of Marie's book reveals much about her personal life, experiences, and philosophy. Despite the considerable limitations of a 1900s-era female, Marie was an anachronism. She progressively cultivated her active, inquisitive mind and burning quest for knowledge through reading, thought, observation, conversing with others, and research.

Marie was highly interested in science – especially in regards to women's issues, biology, anatomy, and health. Marie considered matters of law to prevent and solve problems. She was a woman of modest means due to shrewd investments in land, rental property, and stocks.

Marie were neighbors. Sister Anna Marie thinks that Marie probably journeyed to America with her brother John, who arrived November 3, 1881.

[11] Sister Anna Marie's research indicated the Ellinger Catholic church records showed they were baptized (Catholic) & their names were "Olga Marie" (DOB 11/1887; death 5/1890) & "Marie" (DOB 12/5/1888; date buried 1/16/1889). Sister Anna Marie could not find markers for their graves in the cemetery.

[12] Frances Jez Macik, the daughter of Marie's son, Fridolin Jez, recalled that the surviving children were very close & loved each other.

[13] Sister Anna Marie gathered important genealogy data from her Uncle Norbert Jez, one of Marie's sons. Many of the details provided in the section, "About My Great-Grandmother, Marie Jez" were gathered from Norbert's correspondence to Sister Anna Marie in a letter dated February 12, 1967. The letter Norbert wrote indicated that Marie received a "good education," learned to speak German, and that farming was initially difficult for Marie and Frank since farming was new to them. Correspondence from Sister Anna Marie indicated that later in life, Norbert lived in a nursing home in Sealy, and his brother, Frank Jr., lived in a nursing home in Brookshire (near Sealy, Texas).

Marie received an excellent education from Catholic nuns during the time she spent in two convents. She spoke Czech, German, English, and had some knowledge of French. The reader of her text will be surprised with the depths of her knowledge, as such knowledge was much more difficult to procure for women of her era and circumstances than in the present "information age."

Marie advocated respecting the rights of others. She espoused high ethics and morals. Marie believed people have a duty to ennoble, preserve, and increase the race. She valued life. She was <u>staunchly</u> anti-war. Marie urged others to shape their destinies and live life purposefully - not according to whim or chance. She emphasized that people should learn from mistakes and not repeat them. Marie believed that a guiding principle of life is that each person should strive to "reach his salvation."

Marie held a mixture of traditional and progressive values. She valued the concepts of marriage and family. Marie espoused supportive marital partnerships, equality in marriage, and sound child rearing practices.

She urged men to love and respect their wives, and to use their intellects to assure their wives and children of optimal health by practicing sexual temperance and delay of gratification in order to sire only as many children as could be safely borne by his wife and comfortably supported by the family. Marie revealed that during her era, some women in desperation killed their own children and / or took their own lives.

Marie was a determined child advocate who emphasized that procreation and parenthood are great responsibilities to be approached very seriously, conscientiously, and scientifically. During her era there was a dearth of (a) medical services, (b) educational knowledge, and (c) assistance for children born with serious conditions such as birth defects, mental retardation, and medical problems.

Thus, Marie implored parents to maintain both physical and mental health (e.g., live reflectively, maintain healthy diets, limit alcohol consumption) because she emphasized that the health of the parents plays an important role in procreation.

Marie viewed mothers as the primary educators of children – and not as "servants" to the family. She stressed the importance of formal education, appreciated and supported quality educators, gave behavior management advice (e.g., discouraged permissiveness and use of corporal punishment), emphasized that parents should provide close parental supervision and serve as positive role models, and she cautioned parents to educate their children to resist peer pressure.

She gave health-related advice, served as a midwife, and her book can also be described as a practical "home health" reference booklet for women and their families during the early 1900s.

Marie was an altruist whose mission in life was to serve as a consultant for the common good of others - especially in matters of health and living. She wanted to stimulate thought. She advocated setting goals.

Marie urged others to join her in her mission to encourage all human beings to utilize their intellects for the common good. She aimed to "give my experiences to the world for the good of all mankind, but especially for the good of the female gender."

Marie was a visionary born scores too soon for the conservative climate of the small Texas community and era in which she lived - a divergent thinker and a broad-minded "women's libber" who wanted to change the social structure by empowering women to fight repression.

Bessie Ann Jez Polasek recalled that Marie bravely shared her views with others - even though as a result she was probably harshly criticized, shunned, disliked and perhaps ridiculed by those who rejected her theories and who viewed her ideas as radical and inappropriate.

Nevertheless, Marie unabashedly continued to study and address personal, controversial or "taboo" topics such as philosophy (e.g., the meaning and purpose of life), marriage, health, sex (e.g., she advocated the importance of sexual pleasure for both spouses), and birth control.[14]

Marie had advice for couples to use regarding how to produce the desired gender. Since her gender selection method was believed to be effective for many, and also since she formulated natural herbs and preparations for health remedies, it is conceivable that she was also regarded somewhat suspiciously by others.[15]

Marie's book, originally published in 1926, is entitled *Katechismus Manželů*. The English translation is *A Married Couple's Catechism*. In the book, Marie expressed regret that she would not be alive to witness future world progress.

Her tombstone indicates that Marie died on March 5th, 1930, at age seventy (about four years after publishing her book), in the small town of Wallis, Texas, which is located approximately forty miles west of Houston. Marie is buried in the Guardian Angel Catholic Church cemetery in Wallis.

The reader is reminded that in more modern times, a few of Marie's theories, ideas and thoughts will be perceived as scientifically inaccurate, unconventional, controversial, and some readers may even wince during the reading of particular contents of Marie's book.

---

[14] *Bessie's sister, Clara Jez Hubenak, suspects that some of Marie's ideas may have sprouted from reading the works of Jean-Jacques Rousseau (1712 – 1778), a philosopher who was born in Switzerland and lived in France, as many of her ideas resembled his.*

[15] *Bessie Jez remarked that possibly some may have even referred to Marie as a "witch." Maureen's father-in-law, Sylvester Frank Viaclovsky, knew Marie when he was a child growing up in Wallis. When questioned about Marie, he would only grin & would not share specific recollections – again, the impression was that Marie's progressive activism was not always regarded positively by others.*

For this reason, the reader is reminded to consider the limits of knowledge and the lack of readily available reference resources during Marie's era, and to recall that Marie's intent in publishing the book was generous beneficence, not for personal gain.

~ Since Marie recognized that spoken and written words give humans immortality, she would be pleased that her book survived and her accumulated beliefs and philosophy have been immortalized in this book. ~

Grandmother's Lost, Burned, Banned Book
A Miraculous Find
A short story introduction by Bessie Ann Jez Polasek
December 29, 1985

"Josef, we will have to burn that box of copies of the book your mother wrote. Did you know I caught Bessie reading one?" said my mother[16] to my father[17]. I myself was a child, but old enough to be an avid bilingual reader (Czech and English), somewhere in the 1920's or early 1930's. I accidentally found a Czech book (very controversial in those days – 1920's – as it concerned topics such as sex, marriage, innovative medical techniques, and so forth. It was written by my paternal grandmother – Marie Jez – with an artistic cover which appealed to me. She did not want the book sold for profit so as to avoid litigation if someone was harmed by her advice.

I found the book under a stack of white sheets and pillowcases kept on a shelf in an old-fashioned armoire. My mother probably told me to put away the snow-white sheet which had been soaked in warm home-made soapy water, then boiled, scrubbed, rinsed with bluing, a spoon of salt and baking soda, then hung on the line to dry. Everyone wondered how my mother, a very neat woman, washed the sheets so as to be so white.

I read quite a bit of the book as that small child, but only remembered that when one has a splinter, one should place a hot cloth or something on it in order to remove it with greater ease. Also, I read something completely incomprehensible to my childish mind – "If you wish to have a boy or a girl, you must sleep on the right side or left side of the bed ... "? I did not understand, but thought, "A good thing to know." At the back of the book there was a correction, a printer's error, saying that the "left" side should have been printed as the "right" side...

---

[16] *Veronika (Veronica) Anna Surovcek Jez (born 01/07/1889 in Fayetteville, Texas; died 08/14/1977 in Sealy, Texas)*
[17] *Josef (Joe) Jan (John) Jez (born 03/17/1889 in Ellinger, Texas; died 02/27/1934 in Sealy, Texas)*

The front page in the book had a picture of my grandmother, the author, Marie Jez – a lady possibly in her fifties, with very slightly gray hair which was slicked back, not overly thick - a not-too-thick braid of hair which looked like a crown. The look in her eye gave me the impression of someone somewhat arrogant, as if she knew more than other people and was well aware of it.

Although the picture was in black and white, I recall that her eyes were blue. I hopped up after my mother took the book away, and went outside to sit on the porch, as I heard a train whistle and wanted to see the steam gushing from the smoke stack on the huge engine, and the long load of freight cars. The men on the train waved at us and sometimes threw away a "danger light" (flare) which we rushed to pick up, put in the ground and watch it burn out. Then my dad, mother, older sister and brother and I piled into the model T and went to Wallis to see Grandmother Jez.

In 1979, I finally got a deteriorating copy of the book from a cousin. Why have I been searching for this book all my adult life? I did not particularly like this woman, my grandmother, and I felt she definitely did not like me. Actually, I didn't dislike her, but felt she disapproved of children. Maybe she had reasons. But every time we kids went to visit her, she gave us 50 cents – a generous sum in those days!

I recall that once, as children, my siblings and I sneaked into her garden to pull up carrots. If one was too small, I just stuck it back in the ground. Needless to say, most of the carrots were ruined. My mother caught the brunt of grandmother's ire, and we received a stern reprimand from mother, who was not at all "in love" with her strict mother-in-law.

I remember her saying that when she married Dad, as a bride, they initially lived with Grandmother Jez and Aunt Annie, her youngest child and "pet", and when there was something hard to do such as plucking a chicken's feathers before preparing it for dinner, and Annie was capable and began to do it, Grandmother often said,

"Let Verusha[18] do it!" This was greatly resented by my mother.

On another occasion, Grandmother spent the night at our house, and my young brother Joe[19] and she were conversing. She was trying to instill into his mind her favorite phrase about religion, "God is Air and Air is God."

My mother promptly called from the other bedroom, "Joe, come here." My mother, a very religious person, would not allow Joe to have his mind "polluted" by Grandmother Jez.

In contrast, my mother portrayed her mother[20] as a saint. It was known that Grandma Surovcak worked in a boot factory at one time, and so I remember her fixing some shoes for me. This grandmother was already married when she left Europe and was probably from Bohemia. She bore 16 children, seven females and four males survived.

I still remember the scent of red rose petals (used for tea) drying on a long bench in Grandmother Jez's bedroom – and a glass (dirty) carved with purple decorations sort of like grapes (I have this glass, it is chipped and cracked, but somehow very precious to me in a negative, heart-rendering way with which I would not like to part).

She poured some wine she had made into it for me, and it tasted the best of any wine since, but I could not enjoy and savor it as I kept thinking how dirty the glass was. She was a poor housekeeper ... and my mother said that she made the worst kolaches in Wallis!

Once I was admiring photographs in Grandmother's album. It was on a pedestal, a pretty picture on the cover, covered with celluloid.

---

[18] *Veronika Anna Surovcak Jez*

[19] *Joseph John Jez (born March 24, 1919 in Sealy; died May 13, 1933, in Sealy, Texas). At age fourteen, Joe drowned while swimming alone in a pond near the family home. It was surmised that he struck his head on a rock after diving in.*

[20] *Teresie Tomanec Surovcak (born 04/03/1862 in Vsetin #192; died 06/01/1923). She married Josef Surovcak (born 07/14/1861 in Horni Lidec #11; died 03/15/1942 in Sealy, Texas)*

Behind the pedestal was an open drawer like a partition which contained interesting objects to my childish eye – hat pins, dress pins – but what really appealed to me – that I had never before seen in my life – was a small gold thimble. It fit my little girl finger perfectly. "I must have it," I thought.

Mother practically raised us inside the church so my conscience told me that I must ask permission. One of the Ten Commandments we repeated in our evening prayer before going to sleep was, "Thou shalt not steal." So I asked, "Grandmother, may I have this thimble?" "No," she said.

However ... I did take the thimble, and promptly, "sure as shootin," Grandmother sternly reprimanded my mother that she "was raising thieves." I don't remember whether I had to return it (which I am positive mother would have compelled me to do, or if I denied it, of course mother would have sided with me). Maybe I lost it. I cannot recall. This episode made a profound impression on the remainder of my life. In fact, in adulthood I became a highly trusted employee at the Wallis State Bank in Wallis, Texas, and also an officer who knew the combination to all the vaults, and about the handling of the right of depository.

As a young girl, Grandmother Jez joined a religious order[21] and was a nun, but could not get along for some reason - perhaps because of her strong views. But she liked the nuns, and said that, "nuns are good but priests are swine!" She recalled that once while she was in this convent, a priest gave her a lot of penance[22] and then laughed about it. For some reason she left that convent and joined another order.[23] But the Mother Superior nun, upon

---

[21] *Austrie Hungaria Notra Dome Pozoney – believed to be a cloistered (secluded, monastic) order*
[22] *prayers to recite after confession of sins*
[23] *The second convent was called "Viden" or "Venia". Perhaps she was told to leave due to her outspokenness – for example, her derogatory comment about priests may have been overheard & caused her to be ejected from that convent. Also, Bessie Jez Polasek and Clara Jez Hubenak recalled hearing that Marie confessed that she had been in a previous convent (to a priest during confession) and that perhaps, to her detriment, the priest then shared this confidential*

checking her garments, discovered the other order's name on them, and when they saw that she had been a nun in another order, it seems that they did not allow her to stay.

I believe that the convent was where she learned fluent German. It is also conjectured that she learned German while working in a flour / wheat mill. So Grandmother was fluent in Czech, German, and also knew a little English and French.[24]

Under what kind of circumstances she met Grandfather Frank Jez, is unknown. He was an excellent carpenter (like St. Joseph). Parts of the house he built in Wallis still stand as it was built with square nails and thus would be very difficult to tear down.[25]

---

information. If she believed this to be true, this could also account for her anger (perhaps unjustified) at some priests.

[24] *The good education Marie attained in both convents undoubtedly contributed immensely to her lifelong quest for additional knowledge. In her book Marie describes gaining knowledge through reading & conversing with others. Clara Jez Hubenak recalled being told by her Uncle Adolph Krchnak, that Marie also attended meetings of a "Freethinking" or "Freethinker" intellectual society in the neighboring town of Rosenberg, Texas, accompanied by a friend. The good friend was probably M.F.K. Cerny, who wrote two sections in Marie's book. Some of the genealogical statistics in this book (e.g., dates of birth) were gathered from an impressive work of genealogy entitled The Surovcak Family, which was compiled by Ann Krchnak Schauerte, a daughter of Adolph Krchnak.*

[25] *Marie & Frank's first home was located near the current Brazos High School location in Wallis. After the Jez family left the farm (Frank built the house himself), Marie rented it to Edmund & Frances Chalupa Jurek. (One of their daughters, Henrietta Jurek Pavlicek, was a good friend of Bessie Jez Polasek's. Bessie played matchmaker & introduced Henrietta to her maternal cousin, Henry Pavlicek. Subsequently, Henrietta & Henry married, had 12 healthy children & in 2010 celebrated their 65th wedding anniversary.) David Barta (Henrietta's nephew) recalled that the Jurek family rented the farm from Marie Jez for about 20 years. David also recalled the following: "It was at this house that my mother spent her honeymoon night in the upstairs bedroom ... That is not all ... The bridesmaids slept there also the same night. Mom said there was a lot of giggling going on that night **and it wasn't my dad!**" David's mother was Anastasia "Stasie" Rita Jurek & his father was Theodore "Theo" Charlie Barta (In Czech, "Bohumil Karel Barta"). ...Later the farm was sold to a family with surname "Sowa." Marie's second home (within the city limits of Wallis) was later purchased by Bessie's husband's sister (Frances Polasek Mikes) & her spouse (John Mikes), & thus Bessie & her family continued to visit with relatives within Marie's former house in subsequent years.*

14

Also I remember a carved chair he built. You could not see any nails where it was connected together.[26] It received very rough treatment, the carved spokes[27] where we as children rested or pressed our feet were quite worn, but the chair was not wobbly or shaky at all. Someone in the family has it, I hope. It disappeared from our home.

When my grandparents, Frank and Marie, went to church in a wagon, they often argued along the route. Perhaps that is at least partially why she decided "to heck with it," and quit going to church. But Grandmother made sure all her children were brought up in the faith (Catholicism), and she wanted to be buried in the church cemetery next to her husband.[28]

Grandfather died when he was only 50. I heard a story that at his funeral,[29] an elderly man named Mr. Krecicek continued singing when a song was completed. When the priest told him to be quiet, Marie told the priest to, "let him sing – it was pretty!" Mr. K gave all his money to the church, listened to the priest, finally gave his last cow to the church, became sick, and finally cut his throat because he had no money.[30]

---

[26] *Clara Jez Hubenak recalled hearing that her Grandfather Jez could carve so skillfully that he could make wood appear to be bricks.*

[27] *chair leg supports*

[28] *Clara Jez Hubenak recalled hearing that initially Marie attended church faithfully but Frank didn't. But when he began attending church services, she quit attending. So, Marie became fearful the priest would not allow her to be buried next to her husband in the church cemetery. Vera Jez Hereford recalled that although the priest was hesitant, the priest & Marie's son Josef (Joe) Jez & probably her son Frank Jez also, called the Catholic bishop of the Galveston diocese. The bishop asked if her family attended church regularly & since they all did, the bishop gave his approval to bury Marie next to her husband, Frank Jez.*

[29] *Vera Jez Hereford recalled that this actually occurred at the funeral of Josef's (Joe's) father, Frank Jez, not Joe's funeral. Vera also recalled that Frank Jez died of "stomach trouble."*

[30] *Clara Jez Hubenak recalled being told the following. While Marie was still living on the Wallis, Texas, farm, a neighboring farmer situated drainage so that torrential rains would drain onto her property instead of his. One night during a storm she arose very early & dug a ditch to prevent the water flow onto her land. The next morning neighbors came over - incensed - to confront her. They accused her son, Josef (Joe) Jez, of the caper. Knowing that he had been asleep*

Grandmother sent my dad, Josef (Joe), to San Marcos College in San Marcos, Texas.[31] In those days, Czechs were considered to be inferior (oppression similar to the black race experience), and Joe was the only Czech that dared to go to a school of higher education. Although he had difficulty and eventually dropped out, he learned a lot about electricity.[32]

Grandma Jez was the first person to have a Model T Ford in Wallis. It was steered with a sort of "pilot's stick" instead of a steering wheel. It was one of the first three cars in Austin County in Texas.[33]

In those days, wood was cut with a hand saw, but my clever Dad rigged up a round saw to the wheel of the Model T and used it to efficiently cut wood for people.

& unaware, Marie urged them to go ahead & question Josef. They awakened him & it was obvious that he was sincerely innocent. Marie also wrote a letter to the governor of Texas about the drainage problem, but there was no response. Since she had the ability to communicate in several languages, next she sent the letter in German. Again, no response. Finally, since very few people in Texas were French, she cleverly resorted to writing the letter in French in order to gain their attention. This forced the Austin, Texas, politicians to take the letter to University of Texas professors in order to have the letter translated. Thus, she gained their attention & a ditch was dug to rectify the drainage problem. It is surmised that Marie's request was granted because third party witnesses - university personnel - had become involved.

[31] *Vera Jez Hereford recalled that initially he was sent to a college in Palacios, Texas.*

[32] *Clara Jez Hubenak recalled being told that in college her father Josef (Joe) had difficulty with English composition, but would often assist a non-Czech fellow student with the assignments, and although Joe was not able to pass English himself, the student he tutored did pass! Since the tutored student was not Czech, prejudice could possibly have been a factor. ...Vera Jez Hereford's recollection was that her father Joe did not pass the exam required for a desired teaching certificate because he had to leave school prematurely when his father died.*

[33] *Vera Jez Hereford recalled that the vehicle was purchased from a Sears & Roebuck catalog. When interviewed for this book, Willie Raska, a retired farmer in Wallis, recalled that one of the town's physicians, Dr. Theo Kubricht, an acquaintance of Marie's, bought a car also, & that one Sunday Marie was driving around the church & so was Dr. Kubricht – but in opposite directions. Willie recalled that – alas – the only two cars in Wallis had a collision!*

Dad also made an ice plant and furnished electricity for the city of Needville, Texas (they used kerosene lamps in those days ...), and he later taught his brother to run the electricity for the city of Needville.

He also made his own camera and took pictures at all the local weddings and developed them.

During the depression (the time of silent movies), Dad went around to the Catholic parishes and showed a movie depicting the Passion of Christ. He helped one of his brothers set up a silent movie theater in Angleton, Texas.[34]

He also owned and operated a cotton gin[35] in Sealy, Texas, with his wife's brother as co-owner. (My dad obviously possessed a keen intellect also.)

Sadly, he died at 42 due to illness - possibly caused by traveling some distance - during very cold weather - to repair the roof on his mother's rent house, in an old Model T with no side windows. He became ill either with pneumonia, or perhaps something similar to typhoid – as three other men died similarly around the same time. He died within a week of onset.[36]

On his deathbed, I recall that he told my sisters, Mary[37] and Clara[38], "You all be good little girls and obey your mother." He died about six months after his mother, my Grandmother Jez, passed away.

Not only was Grandmother able to communicate in several languages, but she was ingenious also. For example, she invented an idea for the early model train steam engine. Today it is called a

---

[34] *Vera Jez Hereford recalled that the movie theater was in Damon, Texas.*

[35] *Vera Jez Hereford recalled that it was called the "Jez & Surovcak Gin".*

[36] *Vera Jez Hereford recalled that her father, Josef (Joe) Jez, died of typhoid fever which turned into meningitis & also recalled he died within a week of onset.*

[37] *Mary Jez Ernstes*

[38] *Clara Jez Hubenak*

"cattle guard."[39] However, someone reportedly stole this idea from her.

During the depression, she developed a delicious, nutritious recipe for a soup, but wouldn't divulge the ingredients - supposedly because she suspected that if people discovered that one ingredient was part of a cottonseed, they wouldn't eat the soup. (Cottonseed oil has been used safely and routinely in food for many years now.)

She also had an idea concerning outside roof ventilators which she described to some men who came to see her and who told her they would help her get the patent. She never heard from them again.[40] Of course, roof ventilators are common nowadays.

Grandmother invested some money in a coal mine – I do not know the amount. I seem to recollect maybe a thousand or two (a lot of money in the early 1900s). This was resented as the money could have been utilized by her children. It seems that the certificates were lost, or stolen from her armoire. No one has the name of the mine.[41]

A great deal of Grandmother's medical knowledge stemmed from her morning associations with an acquaintance, Dr. Theo Kubricht. Dr. Kubricht lived close to her home (after she moved to the house within the city limits) and walked past it on his way to his medical

---

[39] *Research by Jane Polasek Connelly indicated that it was elsewhere referred to as a "snowplow" & that, indeed, the idea for the invention was stolen by others.*

[40] *Jane Polasek Connelly's research indicated that the invention idea was actually a chimney vent, &, again, this idea was stolen.*

[41] *Vera Jez Hereford recalled hearing that Marie invested about $1,000 dollars, or $1,000 per child in her family, & that the company she invested in was located in New Mexico. Vera also recalled that perhaps the papers were located in an old trunk at her Uncle Frank Jez's house in Frydek, & that Frank's daughter, Tillie Jez Haedge, told her that the papers were so old & yellow they disintegrated. Jane Polasek Connelly's research indicated that Marie owned $6,000 worth of stock invested in a coal mine in New Mexico (again, $1,000 per child), & that she might have been swindled. Clara Hubenak recalled being told that once when her father, Joe Jez, berated his mother Marie for an investment in stock he believed was unwise, Marie replied, "But when we make money you'll be glad!"*

office. Judging from the contents of her book, her discussions with the doctor often included subjects involving medicine and sexuality.[42] Grandmother probably embarrassed many a person on the Wallis sidewalks by frankly discussing sex related topics.[43]

Why did I have the insatiable desire to find this book, and why am I writing this about Grandmother? I remember her only from when I was a small child. I was only seven years and four months old when she died, and my mother made many derogatory and negative remarks about Grandmother Jez – even after Grandmother Marie died.

But nevertheless somewhere inside me a strong kinship with the positive traits of this domineering, egocentric woman who advocated for women must exist. And as I read her book, am I hearing myself and the voices of millions of women throughout the universe and the ages?

---

[42] *Marie was careful when utilizing the medical knowledge she gained from various resources. For example, in her book Marie reveals that she served as a midwife to others, but wisely advocating summoning a physician for difficult births.*
[43] *Bessie recalled (with humor) being told that her Grandmother Marie Jez hid under the house when she suspected her husband, Frank, would be coming home inebriated & "in the mood" - when she herself was not!*

KATECHISMUS
MANŽELŮ
(A Married Couples' Catechism)

by MARIE DUJKA JEZ

With Introductory Sections
by MARIE F. K. CERNY

Translated from Czech into English
by Bessie Ann Jez Polasek

Edited by Maureen Polasek Viaclovsky

20

TABLE OF CONTENTS

---

[44] *M.F.K. (Marie) Cerny authored the introductory sections to Marie's original book and assisted Marie Jez to publish the book. A letter written by Aurelia Janik Cerny presents a convincing argument regarding the probable identity of Marie Cerny. Please refer to the letter at the end of this book. (Incidentally, the Czech version of Marie Cerny's surname was spelled "Cerna" in the original book.)*

Introduction
by M. F. K. Cerny

A Married Couple's Catechism was written by Mrs. Marie Jez on the basis of her experience and observation, and at her request edited and introduced by M. F. K Cerny, copyright 1926.

This little book was edited at the request of Marie Jez, a woman experienced and compassionate. Mrs. Jez had the opportunity to observe the lives of agricultural working women. Nature endowed her with the gift of reflecting; she did not close her eyes and ears; where there was something to see, she looked, and where there was something to hear, she listened.

When but a young girl, she had the opportunity to observe and realize what life was all about, and ponder which path one must take. When she was young, she married, but her new state and consequent motherhood did not inhibit her intellectual observations. On the contrary, in a certain sense her observations became even keener. So she took the road of a thought which truth she had to first examine.

The result was that when years ago, the news spread all over the world that the Czar of Russia, Nicholas[45], wished to have a son, and if his wish would not be granted, he would divorce his wife[46]. Then the Czarina, in despair, called on anyone for advice.

Mrs. Jez, at that time, was already fully positive of her certain knowledge that whoever desires a son, can have one, and whoever wants a daughter, even that wish can be fulfilled. When the news flashed in the newspapers that the one who could give the Czarina the needed advice would receive a high honor, and the name would become immortal, Mrs. Jez decided to help this couple.

---

[45] *Czar Nicholas II*

[46] *For several years, the Czarina bore only daughters.*

But the ears of the highly esteemed persons who had the power to help her communicate to the Czarina, were deaf. She could not find the route for her advice to reach the Czarina - she found neither the right ear nor willingness. Besides several straightforward refusals, her trust also was misused.

Since she could not find any way to the Czar and Czarina, on the advice of a certain lady, sister of a certain consul, who in the United States represented a certain European power, and with the advice of another person, she wrote a letter directly to the Czarina. As proven by the postal proof note, the letter was given to the Czarina, who bore a son that year, and that was all...

Mrs. Jez did not let herself be timid where people needed help or wanted it[47]. She gave her advice, and in nine out of ten cases, desired results were obtained. Being sure of herself, she wrote to various people to join her in her efforts to help the suffering.

Almost everyone took a negative stance because most of them imagined that an ordinary woman who could barely write should not deem it decent to be attempting to solve such mysteries as determining the gender - unraveling the puzzle. This lady does not maintain to be infallible, but she asks that her theory be more widely circulated, and if someone wishes to experiment, that she not be deprived as the original founder of this knowledge.

She tried many ways and found honest collaborators, but, alas, they could not overcome old and abominable prejudices, undignified for respectable persons, and at the end withheld their help from Mrs. Jez. Seeing that she could not count on these prominent people, she decided to collect her experiences in this booklet. But even here she could not reach her goal. Finally, after I personally made her acquaintance, and after hearing about her disappointments, slights, and bad treatment, and after she gave me proof, I decided to do this task myself.

---

[47] *regarding desired gender of a child*

In this booklet you will find written all her experiences and views. At the present time there is much talk and listening to people's pitiable thoughts that all this ignorance is disgusting, not only to the masses, but also some educated people. One likes to lend an ear even to an ordinary person if the person wagers his life and death on them. Especially if one realizes that this lady is not driven by fanaticism but attempts somehow to help those who need help, and she does not force her beliefs, but wishes for the good of the experimenter that everything be taken in good faith.

Of course Mrs. Jez does not agree with all things in the knowledge of this day and age, but very little if any of this am I including in this book. Often many things seem different in theory than in practice. I myself cannot agree with everything Mrs. Jez says, but on the other hand I became well acquainted with her and realized that in all living things there are certain laws in which variations are merely accidental.

It is a definite fact that human beings give to everything else more observation, interest and thought than to their own hereditary beginnings and reason for existence in this world. Therefore with gladness I began this work, even though everyone may not agree with the thoughts and experiences of Mrs. Jez. Anyway, it is possible that a new step may be made toward the real knowledge. And that is why I decided to help Mrs. Jez, because surely she has the right to present her experiences and observations to those who have the opportunity to, and who may want, to hear them.

At the same time, I ask everyone who may find my composition and various expressions erroneous, that they forgive me these faults. But I take it that since my pen was able to express correctly the needs of the people during the World War for winning freedom for our homeland over the sea, I can correctly interpret not only what Mrs. Jez asks, but also for many women and their husbands whose wish it is that their family is growing up or has grown.

Indeed, Mrs. Jez for 36 years has helped many with her advice satisfactorily. It is important to remind ourselves that all evil can be controlled by human endeavor, and it is possible for people to remove or eliminate it completely. This last falls into knowledge which is as yet, at this time, very far off.

For this reason I feel that it is my duty to help Mrs. Jez because it is our duty to ponder - and the good thoughts to keep and the bad to discard. Those thoughts that are to be kept and those worthy of discarding should be determined by our feeling, intellect, and search for opportunity and truth.

Man and Reason for Living in this World
by M.F.K. Cerny

At the beginning of the Earth, man, king of all creation, appeared, and was blessed with spiritual thought, and enjoyed many privileges which exceed by far any other living creature on the Planet Earth. Man probably has no special human weapons; but on the contrary is much better equipped than animals. Sight, fingernails, dexterity, and quickness of body, strength, jumping, running - so endowed are animals above man. Even man's digestive system does not have the ability of double mastication. Against an attack by enemies, a human does not possess natural weapons; nor against cold - wool; or feathers against the heat of the sun; even his instincts are elementary as regards ability to escape from danger.

However, humans possess something much more valuable than all other creatures altogether - a considerably developed brain, from which flows intelligence. He possesses language in syllables, upright walk, and developed hands capable of adapting to a variety of works. He also has the ability to adapt to various conditions of life: can survive on food from vegetation or animals, can adapt to any climate - heat of the tropics or a polar climate.

The main precedence of man that makes him the lord and ruler of the universe is his mental capability, thought and intellect, and expressive language. By means of this expressive speech, a human gives his imagination meaning, and only then is able to become immortal, as he thinks and labors.

He makes thoughts from which emerge deeds and works. These pass from generation to generation. As if the words were alive, they are inherited and spread as statement and legacy in various forms. Or else, how could we call these memorials made by an artistic hand an inspirational thought, which we find after our predecessors?

This is a statement and legacy, and therein the immortality. Yes, with speech a human becomes a human, wise speech thought over, one communicates and teaches, work with his artistic hands creates and this places him above the animal. Since he is endowed with the instinct that what he creates he preserves; thus he rises and is elevated even higher.

Thus, this human endowed with intellect also has a will, which is an independent energy force. How this will is utilized depends on the upbringing. But, according to human laws this "will" should be in the mind to do good to you and thus also to me. Good will should be given to all the human instincts as also to other creatures.

These instincts are really the whole strength of life. Just as they are a blessing on one side to individuals, so they are even to nations a curse. This instinct drives humans to good deeds but also to bad - always and without exception lead to either preserve one's own life or that of his neighbor, or else to oppress, belittle, kill, or eliminate others.

The most highly developed instinct is that of the sex urge. The human is a creature capable of adapting to a variety of circumstances which he himself either does willingly, or is driven by circumstances, he again rises above the animal, exactly because of these capabilities, and to a certain extent can defy human nature.

But, if he does not utilize his intellect and feelings, the characteristics which raise him above the animal, then he brings on himself punishment and demise into which he entangles everyone around him either slightly or to a greater degree. On his circumstances, which place he occupies in a society, depends more or less the happiness and fate of his fellow creatures, either to a small or a large degree.

On this freedom depends all spiritual grandeur, the traits of decency, honor, and capability to improve self; also, improvement in other arts and certain crafts, or other work.

At the same time, dear friend, there is the possibility of falling below the status of an animal. If one gives in to these feelings[48] and passions, not tamed by the laws of the intellect, one falls below the stature of the animal, whose excuse is that the animal does not possess the ability to think with the ability the human from the lowest class can boast of possessing.

The laws of decency are the most beautiful flowers of thought and human ability, because these, with the aid of the human intellect, gave rise to conscience, which, by degree, lifted the human to his present degree of citizenship, and equality of rights, at least on the exterior. The intellect, conscience and will are a person's inner instincts. Deeds and facts are outward acts.

But judging on the basis of reality, according to which I see so much suffering and pain among people, especially in the woman's world, I probably am not too far from the truth if I say this flower, the most precious of all, law of morals, is not practiced as strictly among a large majority, because human life would appear differently. There would not be so many crippled women, poor children, and unhappy fathers.

Worthless remains the faith, all hope changes to disappointment, and all this only because man does not try to develop his intellect, guard over his will, and he yields to his passions, which plunge him below the status of the animal because he has the capability, but misuses it.[49]

Animals, not having these principles, go according to the laws of nature, not possessing the remotest idea that in the world there are any transgressions against nature from not using the intellect that humans possess.

---

[48] *sexual*

[49] *The author surmises that Ms. Cerny is referring to her & Marie's shared conviction that birth control should be utilized so that women do not have so many children that their health is threatened & so that the family does not produce more children than can be cared for adequately.*

The virtues with which a human becomes an equal to the level with gods, and thus could create a Garden of Eden on earth which could not compare with any mythical heavens, because even with all this perfection, one would still stay a human. And after having blissfully used life, a human would depart to his spiritual, eternal sleep with the assurance that one lived as was becoming for a person to live - whose aim in life was doing individual good deeds for his own good, and for the good of others.

The life of a human on the foundation of reality should be the doing of honest work peacefully, with love and joy. It should be the kind of life that glows with peaceful love to all, and with deeds that bring delight and are pleasing not only for oneself, but pleasing to all. And according to one's financial strength, a life where one would happily help everyone to enjoy riches - not only foods, works, entertainment, loving the body - but aiming also for higher aspirations - spiritual treats and enlightenment of the mind, such as searching for truth, and from artistic endeavors and beauty.

From such a creation of an extremely high mind, from the soul and heart of those who endeavored thusly, from this common creature developed a human richly endowed with feelings, conscience, and intelligence. We of course know that every human in today's circumstances cannot give his life this type of meaning. It does not depend on him only, but if all families will strive according to the rules of intelligence, instinct, and law, then, surely, all of us will benefit from being on earth. Even though life may not be ideal, we will get closer to the ideal.

The work of today's man certainly appears to have reached a high mental degree. If also singular families would proceed according to their intellect, feeling, law, decency, then their apparent mistakes would be corrected. Marriage - decent, serene is the blessing of the family, city, state, and nation and a guarantee of happiness of all mankind.

But it is a pity that the dreams that a young bride dreams disappear under the frosty breath of reality, when a happy bride is transformed into a mother who envisions in front of herself a deep dark abyss, and year after year it becomes more terrifying.

Holding her child in her arms she realizes that she has only two choices, to become her husband's slave, or throw herself into the deep abyss with the fruit of her womb. Her instinct of survival, if it is stronger, she turns away from the abyss to give birth again. She cannot defend herself against the foolish passion of her husband, who drowns dignity in his uncontrolled whims, rather than consider that his wife is a sensitive creature like himself.

This man, the lord of creatures, only to satiate his appetite begets creatures while his wife suffers from livelihood work, motherhood, bodily weakness, and the wife-mother is without sufficient strength for the future. This is certainly a sad vision, when we look upon cripples and their mothers deathly tired. This is not the goal of woman, that she would bear against her will so often that under this inhuman burden she will ruin her health and life.

In the human intellect lies the way to use life. To live in poverty and suffering, always skimping and cursing, in tears, then be aware that this is our own fault, and not our fate or destiny. It is a disgrace to be cursing the knife that cut us. Our cut is not the fault of the knife, but our own fault that we used it carelessly. The one who is suffering because of a large family, let him not blame the Higher Will, but blame his untamed passion, brainlessness, and carelessness.

In this book the author[50] presents the foundation based on morals, for the reader to think, try to make discoveries, and experiment on self and others too. Everything is derived from observing life, observing that sometimes foolishly and idiotically life is destroyed, misused, and is ended in great pain when that life could have been lived for the universal purpose.

---

[50] *Marie Jez*

Mrs. Jez, a compassionate woman, would like to reveal her knowledge and experience for the welfare of all wives/mothers for a twofold reason: to be able to avoid conception, and to be able to choose the gender, male or female, of the offspring. And she is presenting her knowledge under the strong conviction that she is speaking to humans of good will, who take or want to undertake life from a serious side, conscientiously, with the inner conviction that a human is called into this world to use this life wisely, cleanly, and in a dignified way.

Only for this reason does she permit her experiences to be written and published.

~ Marie F. K. Cerny ~

CATECHISM OF A MARRIED COUPLE
by Marie Jez
January 1, 1924

Everyone who will read this book, let them not think that I am presenting this book for my own gain. Not so. I firmly believe that I give my experiences to the world for the good of all mankind, but especially for the good of the female gender.

It will deal with so-called private, personal matters, such as the origin of the human body. It is strange that exactly this work[51], one of the most important functions on earth, is not regarded with any kind of consideration - wise consideration, advised by conscience, with feeling and without misconception between the male and his partner. Why, this deed gives life to a third human being with his intellect. So is this not worthy of serious thought? And look, exactly here one deals with careless thought, leaving everything to chance.

I am convinced when I claim, that exactly this false, misplaced bashfulness, shamefully silenced evil thoughtlessness about the importance of this act, lays all the evil; thus humanity, in its progress to achieve, is choked and held back.

For this truth, for this my conviction, in spite that many people may even reject or think ill, I want to tell the world what I observed, saw, and experienced. I only implore everyone individually to forgive me if I should touch upon personal matters. I cannot do otherwise.

If I want to universally and understandingly enlighten, I must take everything into consideration. My conscience prods me, that I must not hold back anything of what accident or chance and my wit gave me to understand for myself, and for the good of many others.

---

[51] *procreation*

I fervently hope, that women - wives and mothers - preserve their health, and that their husbands, where possible, would reach contentment and happiness, their children be their pride and joy, and help them in their old age. I wish that people would work for mutual fulfillment together and get along well.

On the foundation of my experiences I claim, that parents may call into this life the children that they desire. They may choose children of the gender they prefer. And these children will be witty, wise, healthy, and beautiful in body. I believe that this theory will correctly be learned, and humans with two generations will reach such a height that all sages will be astounded.

Yes, this certain important moment[52], which is considered today as a shameful act of humans, decides human characteristics. For this false shame on fulfillment of base senses, the truth is not recognized. As if it would be a shame, that a person must live on earth, and the purpose of his life so magnificent - to improve the world, finish that which nature itself cannot complete, this act of our living. Joy, love, the beauty of work of numerous arts, in these humans can delight and be happy, but only those whose souls are clean, good, and noble.

From my soul I wish that it would be understood what I want to present in this writing - that people produce and bear with informed knowledge, only children who would be good people - beautiful, wise, and thoroughly virtuous.

I myself have read many reflections from experts, but my convictions rest on experience, and do in no way agree with all their ideas. I am strongly convinced that a person doing something should know why, how, and for what reason he does it. And also, that one should do everything, so that he could gain his desire. I point out when one wishes to create something, he must first know how to do it. When he knows this, then he can do anything.

---

[52] *procreation*

It is not said in vain that knowledge is our redemption. A human is endowed with a brain which lets him refine and moderate his various desires, and if he does so, he has the right that his wishes will also be fulfilled. He does not act against his conscience and instincts, never takes away the rights of his fellow men.

In marriage, equality should be above all other feelings, and one should heed the advice of one's conscience - feelings and intellect always should be the judge. The family is the foundation of the state. Both married partners are people; both have their rights but also their duties.

One never is harmed by temperance, and especially in things sexual. An intemperate person is harmful to society, and is even more harmful if he is sexually intemperate. Maybe he does not even realize that he might be calling forth children who are crippled, premature, and retarded - dumping them on society as a heavy burden, and that he is holding back humanity in progress, because thoughtlessly he may beget - if not wicked people - than people who require that others help them in one way or another.

This type of help requires not only time, but also money, which should be utilized for the good of the healthy.[53] How much faster humanity would reach its destined goal! Thus, the married couple should never bring into the world more children than they can support without resorting to heavy sacrifices on their part, and at the expense of the mother's health. There are almost enough people now that if suitably divided, the whole world would be comfortably populated.

Wars are unnecessary - these should be prevented at all costs. A sound person cannot condone the necessity of huge massacres. If the exterminated are not needed here, then they should never have been born, the mothers will not have to bear them in pain, have distress raising them, painfully earn the bread for them, and worry

---

[53] *The reader is reminded that Marie's viewpoint was strongly influenced by the fact that during her era, there was a dearth of medical / educational knowledge & services for the care of persons with special needs. Fortunately, this is not the case today.*

how to provide for their bloodline when they are growing into adult men and women.

Behold then that by war exterminated are the flowers of the male gender - healthy, in the springtime of life, blood is spilled here. The rubbish that stayed at home[54] replaces them. Those that were not killed, are crippled - if not mentally, then sexually, and they beget life and are the foundation of the new generation.

Is it possible to expect the improvement of mankind when the bloodline of the fathers is weakened immediately, or else weakened by rape, which injures the very core of nature?

A murderer for his evil deed is judged, punished – no matter who he murders. In fact, punished would be a person who, on the wish of one suffering from an incurable disease, would kill him[55] - and look - a handful of people decide to hold a war where fall not tens, but thousands of choice, healthy, men. This leader, then, who wins because he could better invent a plan how to kill more enemy men, is hailed, revered in schools and given as an example?

If a simple, plain person kills either from revenge, anger, or another explosively aroused passion, here one could say that he is not responsible for the deed. But when a few leaders decide they will war, they get together and cold-bloodedly plan, I say, cold-bloodedly, so that they could destroy many, healthy, choice people, as many as possible, those leaders are not judged, not even punished!

If honestly there are more people[56] than is possible to maintain, then let women not bear more. What good does it do, all the pain, worry, troubles, when in the end the labor of your life, that child, when he reaches adulthood, is in wars injured?

---

[54] *during war*
[55] *assist with euthanasia*
[56] *on earth*

And what better fate does your daughter await? In daughters are repeated the trauma and also your own. You may have a good husband, but whom will your daughters get?

I bring your attention to this. I do not say that husbands should not beget, but do not beget more than you can rear well for oneself and the world - productive and moral men and women.

It seems that it happens that tens of children enter this world that are undesired even in the mother's womb before they see the light of the day. What destiny awaits this poor wretch? If it becomes a burden to those whose duty is to love it - poor little wretch, who will love it, if its own parents deprive it of natural affection?

Carefully, the master of the household or his wife should not create a larger brood than they can feed and take care of adequately. They would not have any gain. Oh how foolish it is for these parents to bring into the world more children who deserve to be raised decently. Think! You be the judge.

These times are times of freedom, free will with which to plan whatever we want to surround ourselves with; then always let us see to it that we choose for ourselves the best, the most pleasant, that can delight us. But like informed, sensitive people, let us not forget that there are others also, and they also have this freedom and free will, and also this right to do so.

To an informed person, his conscience tells that there are here certain boundaries which his wisdom, sensitivity and sense for life under no circumstances will not allow him to cross over, but there are thousands of those who do not know at all that the words, "I cannot help it," or his, "I want," is nothing more than his weakness, his passions, which lower him and make him a weakling, sometimes to be pitied, other times deserving of punishment.

It would seem that deserving of more punishment would belong where we see that to satisfy "I want," would not succumb only one woman's life, but cause the lack of happiness to a whole line of orphans. What good will pity do here when the passion of man -

with complete understanding of the consequences - wastes again and again at will, ruins health, peace, and essential rest of the woman, forces disease into her embrace, maybe into the grave, leaving with him her helpless orphans? Reflect!

We mothers, who many times do without all sorts of things, know that in self-denial there is a special enchantment that fills one with bliss, and gives one anticipatory pleasure. I presume that I may boldly declare that people who are unable to deny themselves anything in life, never really savor happiness.

A Woman's Purpose

An unusual number of people, even today, fail to realize that they should consider the purpose of a person being on earth. They take everything the way it comes, thoughtlessly. This is a sad situation at the present time, when so many people have advanced so highly in so many departments of knowledge and art, that all of us who are living on this earth could be living here as though in paradise - contentedly, happily, healthy in body and spirit. The noble mind of individuals has already discovered so many aids to the pleasures of life that in reality, to this knowledge it is not necessary to add anything else except that all people should reach all the diverse kinds of knowledge, art, and good will of the enlightened individuals.

So the purpose of life is really that a person should reach his salvation. Whole legions of false prophets, since time immortal, seek this salvation, but in a fashion obviously deceptive. For the fact remains, today people do not arrive at this salvation, because today are dying thousands of women, and thousands of orphans are lamenting the loss of loving mothers, and thousands of men, more or less depressed with sorrow, take the bad luck as a thing that fate, or as some term "predestiny" brings. Barely one out of a hundred husbands thus afflicted, realizes that it did not have to happen, if they would have thought about the relationship between man and nature, which does not allow even the slightest circumstance against nature's laws to escape punishment.

Certainly, woman's nature is to preserve the human species on this earth - but not at the expense of her health, happiness, or even her life. Certainly worthy of sympathy is the wife who cannot bear children. But even more worthy of pity is the woman who does not want children, because dearer to her is her personal comfort, jewelry, kittens, or puppies. Worthy of condemnation is she, who dodges childbearing so she could use all her senses for her own pleasure.

But of all the poorest, pitiful women is she who is made to bear against her will, without the ability to provide for these children. Are not these women humiliated by their own husbands, and thus lower than slaves are?

Does it not make us want to weep when we see a wife who, not so many years ago, was a happy bride placing her hand into her husband's, believing in blissful trust that he will be her best friend and protector? But she, through his fault, is ruined in spirit and body, desperate almost to madness. He, who should be her support, friend, and provider for the family, appears here as a selfish person without interest in the wellbeing of the family. Is that not worthy of pity?

Or at other times we see a woman indifferent to the duties, which were laid at her bosom, from the incomprehension and thoughtlessness on the side of her husband. Not one, but tens of men are like this. They appease their passions, and assert their wrongfully founded drives at the expense of their wives. Many a man considers his wife, instead of a partner, a slave to his whims, a maid to his household, and a caretaker of his children. Certainly, each one of us is familiar with a case where a wife-mother, young yet, took her life "reasons unknown." Or else first took the lives of her children, then her own. Then again, sometimes a man even lost additional wives.

We had the opportunity at one time to visit a hospital. We saw there the pale and bitter faces of women. Did the doctors ever let you look at the various tumors and growths, which were created in the woman's womb, only because they were misused beyond measure and weakened by births and miscarriages? Or else because, introduced into the hearth of the family, was dragged filth from outside[57] through the man's fault? Or we oftentimes meet women with faces of martyrs with a smile on the lips, but a mournful smile. You recognize, surely, of whom is said, "dragging through life" with too numerous a family, their own life ruined.

---

[57] *sexually transmitted disease*

And for what all this? Because the purpose of woman is erroneously comprehended, wrongly interpreted, and exactly by these stronger men themselves. Yes, an individual, a rational being, allows his passions to control his brain. Consideration and spiritual reflection are squelched. Believe me, the saddest image of our time is a wife, mother of man, degraded, her most beautiful ideals ruined. Her faith in her husband's manliness and noble-mindedness, turns into disbelief and disillusionment.

The same once healthy, cheerful, lively, and beautiful girl, now as a wife, if not sent almost into her grave, is put on the operating table to be tended by a doctor. Why? Why? Because he, her chosen one, he, her protector, misused her femaleness to satiate his unreasonable passions. He overloaded her weak breast with birth after birth, not saving her when the fruit of his passion, long she carried under her heart.

Friends, you all know what the word "shame" signifies, right? Well, some sort of tattoos of the word "shame" ought to be shown on the foreheads of all the husbands whose wives are forced to stay in hospitals so that physician knowledge would reveal which husbands sinned against their wives' organs.

Perhaps even the many births would not have had effects on the woman's body if these women would not also have to labor even more than men do. And that is not all, women assume more concerns, cares, worries and responsibilities than men do, and that weakens them even more. Well, and what is needed? *Only if people would let themselves be educated.*

This glass (photographed in 2005), was given to Bessie Jez Polasek by Marie Jez, and is mentioned in Bessie's short story introduction. Estimates are that it was made prior to 1928.

The white "X" depicts the original location of the home of Frantisek Dujka and Katerina Becica Dujka (house number 68), in Slusovice, Czech Republic, where their daughter Marie was born (photo courtesy of Susan Duyka Harrison).

Katerina Becica Dujka (1830 – ~1901) and her daughter Eleonora, circa 1886

(photo courtesy of Mary Dujka)

Marie's parents were Katerina Becica Dujka and Frantisek Dujka. Katerina was born on March 9, 1830, in Trnava (house No. 68). Frantisek was born March 20, 1814, in Lipa, a village (house No. 28), near Slusovice, Moravia (present day Czech Republic). He died March 25, 1879. Frantisek was 16 years older than Katerina. (Unfortunately, no pictures of Frantisek were found.) About seven years after she lost her husband, at the age of 56, Katerina immigrated to the United States from Austria on December 7, 1886. She came through Galveston with her daughters Karolina and Eleonora ("Ella"). Some research gathered by Jane Veronica Polasek Connelly indicated that Katerina traveled to Texas in a covered wagon. In 2010, Kay Bolf Vargus (Eleonora's granddaughter) shared updated information: Katerina lived with Ella and John, who married in Wallis and lived there initially. Then they moved to Taiton, Texas (where they lived about 8 years). She then accompanied them to Leona, Texas, where she died (around 1901 at the age of about 71). *(The preceding information was gathered with the generous help of: Victor Brenk, Mary Beca Duyka, Jane Veronica Polasek Connelly & Karen "Kay" Bolf Vargus, Eleanora Dujka Nezhoda's granddaughter.)*

Frances Dujka who became Sister Sebestiana

Marie's sister Frances became a nun (Sister Sebestiana) and never immigrated to the United States. Like Marie, Frances probably attended grade school in Slusovice and was educated in Catholic convents in Europe.

Initially, Marie attended a convent called "Austrie Hungaria Notra Dome Pozoney Convent," and several relatives believed she followed her sister Frances to this convent. (Subsequently, Marie attended another convent called "Viden" or perhaps "Venia.")

Just before Sr. Sebestiana's mother and sisters Eleonora ("Ella") and Karolina left for America, Sr. Sebestiana gave her youngest sister Ella (who later married John Nezhoda) a small cross-candle holder, which Ella brought to America and which is still treasured by the family.

One of Marie's grandchildren, Tillie Pavlicek Svoboda, lives in Damon, Texas. Tillie's mother was Marie's daughter Olga Jez Pavlicek. Tillie recalled that somewhere around 1940, when she was about 5 (Tillie was born in 1934 – and the family lived in Angleton, Texas then), a fierce storm blew in. The family was very frightened and cowered in fear until the fearfully strong penetrating rain and winds finally blew over. A photo of Sr. Sebestiana was hanging on the wall, and was very damaged by the storm (perhaps much like the photo depicted above). The photo later disappeared.

(Photo courtesy of Susan Duyka Harrison and family history courtesy of Tillie Pavlicek Svoboda, Victor Brenk, and Kay Bolf Vargus, who is the granddaughter of Eleonora Dujka Nezhoda.)

John Dujka/Duyka (1860 – 1931) and
Katherine Kulcak Dujka/Duyka (1861 – 1943)

Marie's brother John was born December 2, 1860, in Slusovice, Moravia (present day "Czech Republic"). He died February 19, 1931 in Hungerford, Texas.

Katherine was born November 25, 1861, in Novy Hrozenkov. She died December 27, 1943, in Texarkana, Texas.

Inexplicably, at some point the spelling of their surname was changed from "Dujka" to "Duyka."

John and Katherine's children were Joseph Stephen Duyka (1885 – 1969) who married Ruth Marie Adamik Duyka (1888 – 1964), Frances Duyka Provazek (1897 – 1969) who married Frank Provazek (1886 – 1972), Frank James Duyka Sr. (1899 – 1978) who married Mary Kapavik Duyka (1905 – 1997), Mary Catherine Duyka Brenk (1889 - 1937) who married Frank Brenk Sr. (1878 - 1954), Philomena / Filomena Angeline Duyka Tyl (1895 – 1984) who married Frank Edward Tyl Sr. (1893 – 1979), Anastasia "Stella" Duyka Tyl (1892 – 1973) who married Louis Tyl (1896 -1963), and John F. Duyka Jr. (1887 – 1967) whose first wife was Eloise (also "Listenas Aloisia") Brenk Duyka (1884 – 1919) and whose second wife was Stella Pechal Duyka (1897 – 1987).

(Photo courtesy of Marie Beca Dujka, wife of Clinton Dujka. Genealogy assistance courtesy of Susan Duyka Harrison, Mary Beca Duyka, Victor & Vlasta Brenk & Elizabeth Pavlovsky Brod.)

Karolina Dujka
(1863 – 1914)

Marie's sister Karolina was born July 8, 1863. Karolina, her mother Katerina Becica Dujka, and her sister Eleonora immigrated to the United States together from Austria on December 7, 1886, when she was twenty-three. They came through Galveston.

Karolina never married, and after her mother left Wallis and moved away with daughter Eleonora and family, Karolina remained in Wallis and lived with her sister Marie, brother-in-law Frantisek, and their children. Karolina died on June 18, 1914. She is buried near Marie in the Catholic cemetery in Wallis, Texas.

Tillie Pavlicek Svoboda, who lives in Damon, Texas, and who is married to Arnold Svoboda, reported that her mother (Marie's daughter Olga Jez Pavlicek) told her that she loved her Aunt Karolina's attentions. For example, they enjoyed examining dresses and other objects that were stored in an old trunk at Marie Jez's home.

Tillie also recalled being told that Karolina died after stepping on a nail (in those days tetanus shots were not routine and many died from lockjaw).

(Genealogy information provided in large part by Susan Duyka Harrison – who also provided the picture – and Otilia "Tillie" Pavlicek Svoboda.)

Anna Dujka Vaclavick (1866 – 1922) and
John Vaclavick, Sr. (1862 - 1947)

Marie's sister Anna Dujka was born March 3, 1866. She married John Vaclavick, Sr. (1862 - 1947) on October 13, 1885, at St. Mary's Church in Ellinger, Texas.

They lived in the Blessing and El Campo, Texas, areas. Available records show that Anna died April 6, 1922, and was buried in Hillje, Texas.

Their children were Helena Vaclavick Cervenka (DOB August 1888; she married Frank Cervenka); Annie Vaclavick Tuma (married Paul Tuma); Henry Kingston Vaclavick, Sr. (1892 – 1959; he married Clara Bercak Vaclavick); John Vaclavick, Jr. (1893 - 1942); Rudolph J. Vaclavick, Sr. (1886 – 1952; he married Annie Malek); Louis Vaclavick, Sr. (~1896 – 1942; he married Mary Faktor Vaclavick); Wilbur Theodore Vaclavick (1903 – 1944; he married Katherine Emma Rickaway Vaclavick 1905 - 1979); and an unnamed deceased infant.

John Sr., John Jr., Rudolph J., and Wilbur and his wife, Katherine, and are buried in Blessing. The *Find A Grave* website lists a Louis C. Vaclavick (with an identical birth date) as buried in both Wharton and Ganado. Old church records show the name as "Vaclavik" but the 1900 census spelling was "Vaclavick".

(Photo and genealogy information courtesy of Susan Duyka Harrison, Mary Beca Duyka & the "Find A Grave" website.)

Eleonora Dujka Nezhoda (1875 – 1962) and
John Nezhoda (1863 – 1944)

Marie's sister Eleonora ("Ella") and her husband John were married in Wallis in 1894, and lived there about two years. Marie and Ella's mother, Katerina Becica Dujka, lived with Ella and John. They moved to Taiton, Texas, where they lived about eight years. Next they moved to Leona, Texas, but stayed there less than a year because they read newspaper ads stating that they could buy land in Texarkana for $5.00 per acre.

At about age 71, Katerina died in Leona prior to the move to Texarkana around 1901. In Texarkana, the Nezhodas cleared about 40 acres and built a home, where they lived about 15 years.

Around December 10, 1916, they moved to a farm in Hubbard, Oregon, to clear land and build another home for their family. Fifty or sixty years previously, that acreage had been a camp ground for lumberjacks, who worked at a saw mill situated on an adjoining farm.

The Nezhodas lived on "Boones" Ferry Rd. in Hubbard, which is historically significant as it is where one of Daniel Boone's grandsons established a ferry to connect travel over the Willamette River. Later his son Jesse cleared a path between Portland and Salem, Oregon, and thus the path became "Boones Ferry Rd."

Ella was one of the first members of St. Agnes Catholic Church Altar Society when it was founded in Hubbard in 1921, and remained active. Ella's husband John became a naturalized citizen in 1921, and was also active in the church. They are buried in St. Luke's cemetery in Hubbard, Oregon in the Nezhoda family plot.

Eleonora and John's children were Matilda "Tillie" Nezhoda Bolf (1911 – 1993), who married John Bolf (1905-1999); Margaret "Margie" Nezhoda Cico Jones (1908 – 1993), who married August Cico (August died in 1939 and later she married Harvey Jones); John Julius Nezhoda (1900 – 1968; single); and Frank W Nezhoda (1896 – 1929; single).

Tillie recalled her mother Ella telling her that just before Katerina and two of her children (Ella and Karolina) left for America, Ella's sister Frances (who had joined a convent in Europe and became Sister Sebestiana), gave her youngest sister (Ella) a small cross-candle holder, which Ella brought to America and which is still treasured by the family.

(Photo & genealogy information courtesy of Susan Duyka Harrison, with family history enrichment provided by Kay Bolf Vargus & Nancy Bolf Flowers, who are daughters born to Matilda "Tillie" Nezhoda Bolf. Kay & Nancy generously shared Tillie's records of the family history, as told to Tillie by her mother, Eleonora.)

Picture of Frank and Marie Jez's home, which was built by Frank, situated on their farmland in Wallis, Texas. The two story section at the back is difficult to discern due to the original photo's condition. Later, the Edmund Jurek & Frances (Chalupa) family lived in the house. Please see footnote 25 for enriching history kindly contributed by David Barta, originally from Wallis, whose mother was Stasie Jurek Barta.

Frank Jez, Sr., working on his farm.

49

One of several chairs built by hand by Marie's husband, Frank Jez, Sr., pictured with their son Josef.

A 2005 photo of one of the chairs hand-built by Frank Jez, Sr., which is owned by Wilhelmina Jez who lives in Sealy, Texas. Wilhelmina's deceased husband, Alois, was born to Marie & Frank's son Norbert (photo courtesy of Jo Ann Hereford).

Marie & Frank Jez, Sr., sitting among their children in front of their farmhouse (left to right): Olga, Annie, Marie, Fridolin, Frank Jr., Frank Sr., and Norbert. Oldest son Josef was the family photographer and thus not pictured.

Marie with daughter Annie

Josef Jan Jez (1889 – 1934) and
Veronica Anna Surovcak (1889 – 1977)

Marie's son Josef and his wife Veronica lived in Sealy, Texas.

Their children were: Louise Jez (1915 - 1915, died in infancy, buried in Wallis), Veronica Frances Jez Hereford (1917 – 1989), who married Joe Miller Hereford (1918 - present), and lived in Sheridan, Wyoming; Joseph Jez (1919 – 1933), the only son, who drowned in a pond near their home; Bessie Ann Jez Polasek (1922 – 1990), who married Charles Paul Polasek (1914 – 2004) and settled in Wallis, Texas; Mary Terese Jez Ernstes (1928 – present), who married Lloyd Edward Ernstes (1920 – 2008), and settled in Katy, Texas; and Clara Ann Jez Hubenak (1930 – 2008), who married Daniel Stephen Hubenak, Sr. (1930 – 1975), and settled in Victoria, Texas. In her later years, Clara moved back to the Jez family homestead in Sealy, Texas, where she and her siblings grew up.

Frank Jez, Jr. (1893 – 1974) and
Mary Hadjik (1897 – 1964)

Marie's son Frank and his wife Mary settled in Frydek, Texas.

Their children were Frank, Mary, William, and Otilia Ann ("Tillie"). Frank (1916 – 1949) remained single and lived in Frydek.

Tillie recalled that her brother Frank had a good mind (e.g., taught himself how to read a Czech newspaper) but died young (around age 33) due to illness.

Mary (1921 – 2010) married Fred Mieth (~1917 – present) and they settled in San Felipe.

Bill (1918 – 2009) married Regina Mieth (~1923 – 2003) and they settled in Frydek, Texas.

Tillie (1929 – present) married Alfred Haedge (1922 – 1972) and they settled in East Bernard. Tillie lost Alfred very suddenly and tragically - at the age of 49 - to a massive heart attack.

(Historical information courtesy of Mary Jez Ernstes, Janelle Mican Barta & Tillie Jez Haedge.)

Fridolin "Fred" Andrew Jez (1896 – 1968) and
Frances Hermina Surovcak (1895 – 1978)

Marie's son Fred and his wife Frances lived in Sealy, Texas. They had four children: Lydia Frances Jez Korenek (1918 – 1997), who married John Emil Korenek (1915 - 2003) and settled in Alvin, Texas (they are buried in Danbury, Texas); Henry Jez, Sr. (1919 – 1981), who married Libby Annie Lubojacky Jez (1922 - present) and settled in Angleton, Texas; Fridolin (Fred) Jez* who married Dorothy Peacock and settled in Foreman, Arkansas (he passed away in 1980 at age 54); and Frances Bernadette Jez Macik (1924 – present), who married Julius C. Macik (1920 – 2007) and settled in Angleton, Texas. [*Genealogy data was gathered with the help of a) Ann Krchnak Schauerte's research in The Surovcak Family, 2001 edition; b) Steve Alvarez' "Cemeteries of Texas" research; c) Frances Jez Macik; & d) Robert Jez (the son of Henry & Libby Jez)].*

In June of 2010, Adam Jez, who is a descendant of Fred Jez and who lives in Foreman, Arkansas, tragically lost his 23-year-old wife, Leslie Jez, and his three-year-old son, Kaden Jez, when a flash flood swept through the family's campsite on the edge of the Quachita National Forest. They were among 20 flood victims. Relatives in Texas keep Adam, other family members, and the families of the other victims in their prayers.

Norbert Anton Jez, Sr. (1898 – 1982) and
Aloisie Pavlicek (1899 – 1978)

Marie's son Norbert Sr. and his wife Aloisie settled in Frydek, Texas, where they are buried.

They had three children: Alois Peter, Annie, and Norbert, Jr.

The oldest son, Alois Peter (1920 – 1993), married Wilhelmina Mlcak Jez (1923 - present) on October 14, 1941 and they settled in Frydek and later moved to Sealy, Texas.

Norbert Jr. (1923 – 1979) married Pauline Pyka (1928 – present) on August 14, 1949 and they settled in Sealy.

Annie Jez (1924 – present) married Paul Henry Saha (1917 – 2003) and they settled in Houston.

[Genealogy courtesy of Susan Duyka Harrison, Mary Jez Ernstes, Wilhelmina Mlcak Jez, Debbie Sodalak Jez, Steve Alvarez, Margaret ("Margie") Jez Toman and Pauline Pyka. The reader is also reminded here that considerable family history was gathered from Norbert Sr. by Sister Anna Marie Vrazel, who spoke with him several times to gather genealogy information. Norbert Sr. also wrote Sr. Anna Marie letters in both English and Czech describing family history. In addition, Wilhelmina Mlcak Jez kindly allowed Jo Ann Hereford to scan several pictures for the other family members.]

Olga Jez (1892 – 1965) and Vaclav Pavlicek (1890 – 1962)

Marie Jez's daughter Olga married Vaclav Pavlicek on December 28, 1913. Initially they lived in Sealy, Texas, then moved to Angleton in 1932, and settled in Damon in 1948. They had eight children: Marie, Edward, Joseph ("Joe"), John V., Adella, Fred, William ("Billie"), and Otilia ("Tillie"). All settled in Texas.

Their daughter, Marie (1913 – 2004), married Donat Vrazel on October 24, 1934, and they settled in Danbury. *(Note: Marie and Donat's eldest daughter, Anna Marie Vrazel is a devout Catholic nun who has been a Sister of Divine Providence since June, 1961. Sister Anna lives in San Antonio, Texas, and reported that currently there are also three priests in the family. She has been a rich genealogy resource for this book.)* Edward C. (1914 – 1989) married Rosie E. Orsak (1915 - 1992) in 1940 and they lived in Damon. Joe J. (1917 – 1998) sustained brain injuries while in the army, was hospitalized for several years, and after that had to be cared for by relatives in Angleton and later Damon for the remainder of his life. John V. (1919 – 1993) lived in Angleton, was married briefly to I. (possibly "Imogene") Smith and never remarried. Adella K. (1921 – 2003) married Vladimir Listak (1920 – 1972) in 1942 and lived in Brazoria; after Vladimir's death she moved to Danbury. Fred (1926 – 1990) married Millie Peters (1921 – 1988) in 1956, and they settled in Needville near what is now Brazos Bend State Park. William (1927 - 1960) married Edna Gardner (who had five children from a previous marriage), and not too long after the marriage William died from injuries sustained in a tragic accident – a fall from height - while working as an ironworker in Tulsa, Oklahoma. Marie and Vaclav's youngest child, Tillie (1934 to present), married Arnold Svoboda (1926 to present) in 1955, and settled in Damon. *(Photo and information courtesy of Susan Duyka Harrison, Sister Anna Marie Vrazel, Tillie Pavlicek Svoboda, and Mary Jez Ernstes.)*

Annie Jez (1901 – 1928) and Frank John Lastovica (1898 – 1972)

Marie's daughter Annie and her husband Frank were married in Wallis, Texas on November 4, 1919, and settled in Needville, Texas. Their surviving children were Joseph John (1920 – 2005), Ellenor Marie (1924 – 1989), and Henry Innocent (1926 – 1974). Annie and their fourth child (Frank, Jr.) died in childbirth in 1928. Mother and infant were buried together in Needville, Texas.

Joseph John ("Joe") Lastovica was born in Wallis, Texas and married Gladys Lyde Martin Mercer on July 2, 1949, in the Base Chapel at the US Naval Station in Argentia, Newfoundland, Canada. After military service, they lived in Houston and then El Campo, Texas until his death in 2005. Ellenor Marie Lastovica Bergeron Bowden was born in Sealy, but lived and died in Houston, Texas. She and her first husband divorced, and her second spouse was Josh Bowden, who died in 1982. Henry Innocent was born in Needville (1926 - 1974), and married Edith "Marjorie" Needham Lastovica (1921 – 1992) in Houston in 1949, where they lived. Marjorie was born in Derbysire, England.

After his first wife died in 1928, in 1931 Frank married Frances Pavlicek (1912 – 1997) in Frydek. They had one daughter, Margaret Lastovica (initially she was married to Mr. Alvarez, her second husband was Mr. McLean). Frank and Frances were buried in Frydek.

[Many thanks for genealogical information provided by Susan Duyka Harrison, Mary Jez Ernstes, Steve Alvarez (the son of Margaret Lastovica), and Rose Ann Lastovica Cook (the daughter of Joe Lastovica).]

Willie Raska, a retired farmer in Wallis, provided this picture of Marie's car and the following recollections: Marie owned the first car purchased in Wallis, Texas, and the third car in Austin County. The other two cars were owned by Doctors Kubricht and Mize. One day two of the three proud car owners (Marie & Dr. Kubricht) were traveling around the church – but in opposite directions. Willie recalled that – alas – the only two cars in Wallis had a collision! Pictured in Marie's car are Willie's mother, Mary Hajovksy Raska (on left), and her future sister-in-law, Anna Raska Kostalnik.

Marie Jez, proud car owner … who appears to be pretending to be a "Speed Racer" in her Model T. Marie's granddaughter, Vera Jez Hereford, recalled that the Model T was purchased from a Sears and Roebucks catalog. *(Photo provided by Wilhelmina Jez and reproduced by Jo Ann Hereford).*

After she had been widowed for several years, Marie moved from the farm (in Wallis, Texas) to this house (photographed in 2005) within the Wallis city limits. Later, the house belonged to Bessie Jez Polasek's sister-in-law (Frances Polasek Mikes) and her husband (John Mikes).

Bessie observed that, *"A great deal of Grandmother's medical knowledge stemmed from her morning associations with ... Dr. Kubricht. Dr. Kubricht lived close to her home ... and walked past it on his way to his medical office. Judging from the contents of her book, her discussions with the doctor often included subjects involving medicine and sexuality. Grandmother probably embarrassed many a person on the Wallis sidewalks by frankly discussing sex related topics."*

Marie Somer Cerny (1858 – 1923)

The two introductory sections to Marie Jez's book were penned by "M. F. K. Cerny," and reveal that this person was instrumental in facilitating the original Czech publication of Marie's book. For several years, this author pondered M. F. K.'s identity. The only clue was that at the end of her written contribution to the text of the book, M. F. K.'s name was listed as "Marie F. K. Cerny". *(Many thanks to Frank Foltyn and his brother for related translation assistance at the request of Aurelia Janik Cerny.)*

Fortuitously, while reading a *Wallis News Review* dated September 18, 2003, this author spotted an interesting story about members of the Fort Bend Heritage Society arranging for a historical marker to be placed at the Krasna Settlement cemetery, on the outskirts of Wallis, Texas. The article went on to describe history reported by Jerome Cerny: *"... In 1893, my grandparents Vaclav and Maria Somer Cerny sold their 160 acre farm in Nebraska, after near starvation on land that he acquired through a land program offered to immigrants from Europe. The family of nine traveled for several months by horse and wagon from the panhandle of Nebraska ... and through Texas settling at Krasna, joining some of their friends. His life was cut short, after only nine months of being a Texan, he suffocated in a water well on his 646-acre farm he purchased shortly after he arrived in Krasna...."* The article continued, *"Vaclav was one of the first settlers laid to rest at Krasna ... On Saturday, Oct. 11, 2003 at 10:00 a.m. the community will gather at the Krasna Cemetery on B.J. Dusek Road for the dedication of a Texas Historical marker for the Krasna Settlement...."*

The author saved that article, and some time later when she resumed working on this book, she reached out to a cousin, Joan Marie Viaclovsky Whiclep Reuss, who grew up in Wallis and knew several Cernys. Joan Marie led the author to Simon Cerny and his wife, Frances, who led the author to their sister-in-law, Aurelia Janik Cerny. Aurelia, in partnership with her husband, Jerome Cerny, had already done extensive genealogy work on the Cerny family, and was instrumental in acquiring the historical marker for Krasna. (Sadly, prior to the author contacting Aurelia, Jerome Cerny had passed away.)

Aurelia investigated and soon presented a convincing argument regarding the probable identity of "M. F. K. Cerny" as "Marie Somer Cerny" (DOB 12/16/1858), the wife of Vaclav (later changed to "Wencel") Cerny (DOB 10/27/1853). (*Note: Marie's maiden name was spelled "Sommer" on some documents.*) Please refer to Aurelia's convincing letter of explanation, dated 11/8/05, at the end of this book. Additional information about Marie Cerny follows, which was gathered from Aurelia Janik Cerny's comprehensive and impressive genealogy work on the Cerny family, entitled *CERNY SOMER ROOTS IN CZECH REPUBLIC*, self-published in 2000, and again in 2005.

Marie and Vaclav had eight surviving children: James, Anna, Mary, Antonie, Agnes, Rosie, Emily, and Frank. The first four were born in Europe. Agnes, Rose, and Emily were born in Nebraska, and Frank in Texas. James was born in 1878, and married Louise Viaclovsky Cerny. Anna Cerny Jurek was born in 1880, and married Joe Jurek, Senior. Antonie was born in 1884, and died in Europe. Mary Cerny Schiller was born in 1884, and married John Schiller. Antonie Cerny Kulhanek was born in 1886, and married S. W. Kulhanek. Agnes Cerny Grigar Martisek was born in Nebraska in 1890; her first husband was Robert Grigar, and her second husband was Joe Martisek, Senior. Rosie Cerny Grigar was born in 1891, and married Louis Grigar. Emily Cerny Klecka was born in 1893, and married Steve Klecka. Frank Wencel Cerny was born in 1895, and married Louise Dusek Cerny. *(Aurelia's husband, Jerome Cerny, was one of the children born to Frank and Louise.)*

Aurelia Janik Cerny and her husband Jerome are acknowledged for their important contributions (including the picture of Marie Cerny). Thanks also to Frank Foltyn and his brother for translation assistance at the request of Aurelia. It is also important to acknowledge the important contribution of Joan Marie Viaclovsky Whiclep Reuss, who led Maureen to Aurelia.

Bessie Jez & Charles Polasek

Bessie, whose father was Marie's son Josef, worked determinedly to translate Marie's book from Czech to English, and authored an introduction, which is included in this book. Her husband, Charles, assisted with the translation. In addition to Maureen, Charles and Bessie had three other children: Larry Polasek of Sante Fe, Texas - married to Judith (Thibodeaux) Polasek, Jerry Lee Polasek of Sugar Land, Texas - married to Sue (Hye Ok Cho) Polasek, and Jane Veronica (Polasek) Connelly of Houston, Texas – married to Charles Connelly.

Marie and her husband, Frank, are buried in the
Guardian Angel Catholic Church cemetery in Wallis, Texas.

Rights of Men, and their Wrongdoings

Before a man wishes to get married, he should first ask himself, "Do I want and I need a wife for a companion, a mother to my children, or will I be forced to make her a servant, laborer in every type of work? Will it be possible for me to leave to her solely the jobs of housekeeper, cook, and caretaker of my children and myself?" And not only that, he must go farther and dig even deeper into his mind - he should tell himself, "And should she be my partner, this future mother of my children, or only a slave to my passions, lightening rod of my mood, and servant of my rule?"

Yes, men have their rights, which nature gave them, but also they have their duties. If they wish to fulfill their passions, have a slave to their every notion, then, they are overstepping those rights. They lighten their duties, becoming, briefly, unworthy of the name "man"! Every husband has the right to ask his wife to be a good housekeeper, cook, and to ask that she understand her household and everything which its outcome entails. He also has the right to request that she become the mother of his children, but only when she is physically able to be a mother.

It is in the woman's disposition that almost all long for a child or more. Surely very few this longing lack, and each one gladly accepts this motherly labor on herself. But before a man has the right to request, he should be respectful, thoughtful and compassionate. He should know that a woman, to become the mother of beautiful, healthy children of body and mind, must not be permitted to be misused by heavy, physical work, or lack good nutrition, or be abused physically and by mental cruelty of all sorts.

It is a shame of our time that the wife of a farmer or laborer, even though the husband be ever so conscientious and good, is in poverty, must not only be his helper and housekeeper, but must help with his labor. These are due to circumstances, when the reward for work does not balance in money for the husband's hard labor.

Human society is at fault, causing the woman's poverty and suffering, but the man's duty is to attempt to better the circumstances and establish compensation for his work to equal the expenses that are average for an adequate livelihood for family life, and that also something would be left over for old age, so that the wife-child bearer, receiver of the breed, would not have to suffer.

Since we know that thus far we are unable to level circumstances, that a woman is forced to - even against the will or wish of the husband - to labor with him, here the husband should have enough consideration toward his completely devoted partner not to force her into motherhood. Indeed it is from the husband not only absurd, but most cruel to induce his work-run-down wife into the state of motherhood more than three or four times.

It should, properly speaking, be a man's shame when his wife does not wish to bear, but is forced to against her will. Indeed it is a shame that women-mothers fill up hospitals and are dying, leaving behind five, six, or even more orphans. Do you not think that in this men are committing a horrible injustice? They perhaps do not realize this. We all have much to learn before we become benevolent people.

Yet, we cannot do otherwise than directly approach truth and man's erroneous view, or their presumed "rights," and fearlessly disclose the meaning of "rights." Because, these are not "rights", but simply an executing of injustice which destroys a woman bodily.

The children who enter this world, not even of their own volition, are wretched creatures. They grow up, these orphans, usually without love, without attention, without order, and without education - thrown on the recourses of an accident. And is this right? Is this wise? No. On the contrary, it is highly coarse and inhumane. There are enough misfortunes which are impossible to avert.

When through the fault of the husband a young wife-mother dies, or from many childbirths an overloaded and damaged woman is forced to go to the hospital, that is the sign of shame for the husband. It appears here that he is the slave of his animal instincts, that he succumbs to his uncontrolled passions without regard for the health and safety of his wife, without regard for the well-being of his children, and without regard for the contentedness and peace of his household. Appears before us here a creature who freely chose to step lower than any animal.

It is worthy of your thought, because through the fault of these particular men, the jails and insane asylums are filling up, receiving their share. As if there were not enough misfortunes for which not any of us is responsible.

Injustices Committed to Children Born and Unborn by Intemperance of Men and Ignorance of Mothers

Gravely sin men on their descendants when they misuse their strength by squandering it. Often they squander their health so that they lose it. Other times various lewdness, drunkenness, or ignorance cause them to end up with various diseases which then reduce their bodily strength for their descendants.

Sometimes, also, indeed very often, a husband, in an unpleasant mood, dissatisfied with the whole world without deliberation, asks his wife to have intercourse. Woe, three times woe, if she permits, and he impregnates her! Wretched then is the descendant for his whole life.[58] Unhealthy and poor, he does not find happiness in anything, nor satisfaction.

More awful is it when the father is afflicted with some bodily disease, and in that moment calls a child on earth. Let everyone well realize, before he wants to become a father, is he capable of calling to this world descendants who are healthy, intelligent, and lively?

If a person cripples someone, body or mind, he will not escape punishment, or a fine. But when a man sires a cripple, bodily or spiritually encumbered child, usually for this ill fortune he is pitied. He is pitied but he should sooner deserve punishment for it, if he called to life a descendant during a time when he himself felt unhappy or unwell.

Where then is his manliness, his wisdom, his sensibility, when he gives way blindly to his lust without regard for the happiness and contented life of his own child? After all, the child is the fruit of his marriage. If the human race would not be propagated, for what reason would we live here?

---

[58] *Because the father was in an undesirable mental or physical state during procreation*

No person ought to go into marriage solely to appease his sexual lust without punishment. Nature does not permit any one of her creatures to overstep her laws. If a person would obey nature's rules, he would not be caught with degenerate impulses, he would not be forced to appease his passions, which overcome his humanity and his brain, and cause unhappiness to the fruit of his marriage – his children.

Often we hear people say, "Horrors, he sins," or "He will be punished for his sins," and so forth, but no one sins more than the man who gets inebriated, and in that state, asks his wife, or forces her to bid his wishes. This sort of man is worse than an animal. Poor woman, if at that interval she becomes pregnant, because she may then involuntarily give life to a wretched child, mentally impaired, who from infancy becomes a family tragedy and ends up in an insane asylum, and the mother may only have the consolation that the child did not end up in the gallows.

No less condemnation-worthy, is the kind of husband-father, who before he married, paid homage to a filthy[59] life, and with this was infected[60], and then after marrying an upright and clean woman, asks her to bear him healthy children. That type of man is exactly like an animal. Not only does he cripple his wife, but also his children - long before he sired them, he robbed them of the sap of life.

That kind of a person, mindless, is a creature heartless and without conscience. Every young man should be educated to take care of his health, as on this foundation will one day be his life insurance. Not only is this his duty, but he should with deeds preserve his health.

If he oversteps sometimes the laws of nature, then any punishment which he receives, he deserves. But never is he punished alone, but others, innocent, with him must suffer.

---

[59] *promiscuous*
[60] *with a sexually transmitted disease*

In particular, fathers should bear in mind not to misuse alcohol. When they cannot resist this passion, then during the time of being under the influence, may they not engage in procreation with their wives. When a child is conceived at this time, under the influence of alcohol, it surely carries the evil fault of his father in itself.

This child, even if it were perfectly reared and did not have the opportunity to imbibe in alcohol consumption, yet, at the first opportunity it will fall for his father's mistake. He gets drunk, although he knows that it will be his downfall. Rebuke, threats, and pain do not help. Perhaps for a while he avoids drinking then more heavily falls into ruin. Unhappy are such families where the father drowns his good name and the reputation of his whole family in alcoholic drinks.

I will tell you a certain event. A certain man was a big alcoholic. He already had two fair daughters and two sons. One lady asked the alcoholic's wife, "How does it happen that although your husband is a drunkard your children are decent people?" She answered, "My dear lady, even though my husband is whatever kind, he had enough feeling for the rights of others, that when he was in the state of intoxication he never asked that I yield. He always said that he did not want children like himself, and he alone knows what torture he has suffered."

Well, then, with other faults of fathers, it is the same. If his blood contains something harmful, then one should not marry at all. As far as I'm concerned, I would approve every law that protects bodily and mental cleanliness in humankind. It is a shame that even today in the 20th century, prisons, asylums for the insane, deaf, blind, and also hospitals must be built. Why? Because these buildings are the proof that people, in spite of recognition of their own dignity, rear their young in an improper manner. Do we observe animal descendants, whether many are impaired?[61]

---

[61] *The reader is again reminded of the dearth of medical & educational care for persons with serious special needs during Marie's era. Fortunately, this is not the case today.*

But before I finish this chapter, I must ask, "Are men directly or indirectly responsible for their faults and wrongdoings, which later on their wives and they commit?" They are responsible, but not directly. Although they brought their faults into the world and, it is true, as an inheritance from their fathers, and from habits and superstitions of their mothers, so, alas, they did not know better.

A mother is not, and should not be only bearer of his children; she must also be their instructor. Toward this task she is adequate, but barely 10 from a possible 100 mothers are able to devote themselves to this task. Lack of knowledge, and then circumstances, are the causes that mothers cannot rear their children intelligently, because they do not know *how* to rear a successful person.

A chronic wrongdoing by almost all mothers is that they allow their children to associate with others together, without realizing what they are, as a matter of fact, doing. Usually they meet without wise supervision, they do there whatever enters their minds, and surely there are among them those who already know more than they should, and also know of many unvirtuous acts. Rampant then are appeasement of sexual impulses near adulthood in a manner unnatural, and long after a boy can become a father, or girl a mother, perhaps already performed were deeds in fact dangerous - provoking sexual impulses without knowing what they are. As a matter of fact, they do not know what they are doing.

To this type of activity are led children by the thoughtlessness and lewdness of adults who do not pay attention that often they are watched by their children, or else they do not care in the least. Parents should always be mindful that to all they should be an example praiseworthy of imitation from their children. The most common result of this kind of improper forgetfulness is premature stirring up of the sexual nature, which then throw youth of both genders either into premature licentiousness, or into sickly spiritual state.

Also, through inappropriate clothing, diet, and other circumstances, children have damaged or mistreated sexual organs, which often without visible example, tempts a child to execute actions that are opposite and directly against laws of nature. Small clothing in the crotch, narrow shoes, cold feet, and other seemingly trivialities restrict free blood blow, and are enough in a growing body to cause unpleasant disturbance from which, with the passage of time, arise consequences sufficient to decay the health of an individual or a whole family.

Another time, as I mentioned above, these excitements are aroused by unwise parents directly. Our mothers, unless informed by reading, to this day do not recognize nor understand the laws of nature any more than the mothers during the time of Moses. Yet instead of science and intellect, they take refuge in superstitions. And this addiction and evil among women does not decrease!

Why? Only why? Because they themselves do not better educate their children. I heard not once, but a hundred times, women lamenting about the insensibility and coarseness of husbands. Yet do they strive themselves that their sons would some day be better? A sensitive person has the consolation that the never ending, always pushing ahead development of everything human becomes better and better. But it progresses very slowly, and a human lives here only a few years. And to many of these women in their suffering, even this short time appears to be an eternity.

How could a lad grow up to be a sensitive, conscientious, and considerate man, when before adulthood he is seduced into destructive habits? Should not the mothers carefully supervise their children? Would it not be more thrifty than later all the various doctor bills? Is there any task more holy than the duty of a motherly education? Mothers are created for this purpose.

Supervision, observation and science should be guided with knowledge sensibly. Only this manner is expected by nature. When the mother observes something, she should caution and not find it necessary to explain. Nature entrusts a child, clean and innocent, into the lap of parents. Well, then, if they have intelligence and enough moral foundation themselves with their actions, they will not lead their children's minds into improper thoughts. They surely can lead the child to his bodily and spiritual maturity without accident and various disturbances. If they accomplish this, then they completed the task without fault.

Until 16 or 17, a boy should not be aware than he is a male for anything else than to become bodily strong and healthy, so he could help his father or devote himself to some other occupation. The son should be led to study, to work, to reflect about useful things. Physically he should be capable of being a father but absolutely not become one, because there are several years necessary for him to grow strong and tough for work.

On the mother depends that the boy is taught that for his immature body, sexual misdemeanors are to be avoided - a downfall upon which later nature without mercy judges and imposes punishment, and he will later be bitterly sorry. This is not difficult when the mother reminds herself that it is in reality her duty. When the mother asserts her will, she will never disappoint her child, always tells him the truth, and thus if even the child had an inferior father, in spite of this he will mature into as kind a person as the mother's influence allowed.

What mothers most permit[62] is what, in the eyes of their children, lower the mother to merely a nursery maid in this matter. And I lay emphasis on her, because only then will begin reparation, and improvement of man will follow. That is, no mother has the right to demand respect, obedience, and gratitude from her children if she did not instill and nurture these virtues in them. Of course, if there are no better women to do so, then the world must educate the people.

Mothers greatly err when they fulfill a small child's every wish - when every one of his pleas must be granted. With these fulfillments the mothers are plaiting a whip for themselves. However, when they want to appease the child only with promises,

---

[62] *permissive parenting*

even though they do not intend to keep them, they are lowering themselves into liars.

An infant screams. Mother's duty is to investigate *why* it screams. It is necessary to observe if it is screaming from a visible reason. If it is screaming only to be screaming, then if a stern look does not help, we must let it scream. Never unnecessarily pick up the child.

An important duty is that the mother should know what to feed the infant. On this correct beginning, its whole future rests. To the infant belongs mother's milk, and during the beginning it should not be fed anything else. If the mother does not have milk, she should seek the advice of a doctor, or seek advice from an experienced woman. But whether the milk is the mother's or a cow's, it should survive only on milk up to nine months.

An informed mother should not regard her motherhood in a nervous manner. When she teaches her child routine when breast feeding, and treats herself intelligently, she does not even feel that she is providing livelihood for the child. The infant will not torment her at night with crying, and will not have indigestion. It will have regularity, and this is the first step to good habits that will never abandon the child. If the infant is fed something other than milk the first year of its life, either it may become a glutton, or his digestive system suffers, and this is not the child's fault - this is the result of the mother's volition.

Then when the child is older and has an inclination toward stubbornness or tantrums, let the mother ponder well what she wants to do, as sometimes it is really hard to do your own will. She must be a prudent judge, and carefully apply what she distinguishes – and if the child's wish is legitimate, to grant it unless she is unable to grant it in the present circumstances. Never, then, should a mother thoughtlessly humor the whims of her child. But when once she makes a promise, she should fulfill it. Promising, and not fulfilling, is dishonest.

The child who some day will grow up to be an adult, a dutiful being, must know how to obey. This it does not learn from beatings, but from exemplary models, and in the primary place, from parental example - mainly the mother herself. This includes avoiding scaring the child with ghosts or otherwise, so that it would behave from fright.

Epilepsy, heart trouble, asthma and so forth may have their beginnings from such parental absurdity. These disorders then have an influence in the character of the person. Even the less witty should understand and avoid them. Additional treatise really does not belong in this book, therefore, I end this little chapter with an entreaty that everyone think over and reflect upon whether it is in their power to add something that would contribute to the improvement of mankind.

Parents, ponder well that the bodily growth of youth needs proper care - that young strength reveals various signs by which is distinguished the transition from childhood to young manhood and womanhood, and that these frighten the young person. Painful is the admission that exactly in these important living times, usually the youth steps without advice and guidance of parents. Honest, moral, and conscientious parents here are afraid of their duty. They do something that punishes the parents and children equally. They forget to make their children their trusting friends, their most true partners.

From this want of confiding flows immeasurable evil, which brings ruin to nations. Reflect! Not any property, no pleasure, no surplus, can retrieve trust of children to parents. If parents would bury their children in gold, this could not replace the parental trust, knowledge, and intelligent support that could have been theirs through the road of life. Instead of permitting the *world* to do so, the *parents* should educate their children and then good will be on earth. Peace, luck, and abundance flows only from our leadership and our work. I cannot yet conclude this chapter, in order that I again return and bring attention to a certain case that concerns education of children.

74

I point again to this, that children must not be permitted all their whims. A child is like a young sapling, from which we someday want a useful tree. We must cultivate it, water it, and useless limbs or various crookedness[63] avoid. A child must not be permitted everything, but over this must be given partial free will, which, however, must never be opposite of mother's or father's instruction, or be made lighter. Nevertheless, to punish children too much, and especially unjustly, should not be done.

Where there are more children in the family, and through someone's fault something is lost without the mother knowing who committed the loss, she must inquire. It is, after all, clear that a child afraid of being whipped sometimes denies or blames another.

In this type of situation, the mother realizes that she is not all-knowing, so she can show that she could punish all who were present. However, she realizes that the transgressor did not commit the damage on purpose, so she will forgive, but make it clear this must never be repeated. She must compel the child to assure her that this would never be repeated, and to thank her that she did not impose corporal punishment.

Those that were not the transgressors will gladly approach her with a promise that they will be careful. The guilty one will not be treated so lightly, because companions know that he did it, and his conscience will prevent him from trustingly approaching his mother. In the event the mother is sure that a child is committing various harmful deeds, then she must carefully watch over him and not forgive punishment even once. Then, punish the transgressor out of the sight of the others, so they would not see him humiliated.

During the nurturing of children, it is necessary that the parents hold the children's respect, trust, and faith that their parents are not only their bread winners, but their best friends, and the most honest people that ever lived on earth. And therefore they must, in the minds of the children growing into adults, appear as if they are

---

[63] *less desirable traits or disorders*

able to bring their children the blue from the sky - but this blue they do not want or choose to bring, to avoid spoiling the child.

A certain lady had a child and was, of course, forced to discipline it. She observed that she began to lose the child's trust, and she felt sorry for that. She decided not to punish the child. Her children, however, did not listen to her words, and always did something that displeased her. That she was a wise person we realize from this: she was thinking it over, and decided that whenever they committed some wrong, they must beg her or the father to forgive the deed. That was something they did not want to do, but they had to. But when they committed something more, then they did have to receive a spanking and also then had to say, "Thank you," for the spanking. This was something highly undesirable and cured them of naughtiness.

All children should attend school, so as to learn useful things for life. Parents should endeavor that the children learn really useful things in school - morals, love for neighbor, economizing, and knowledge of nature and about human relations - and not about fairy tales and how and where someone excelled over others in brawls or wars. Erroneous school education leads youth to a light-minded[64] life and to a superficial way of looking at things.

Teachers should be older people, worldly-wise, and intellectually endowed. They should see to it that the children learn punctuality, and when he or she has a breathing spell, the teacher should observe the children's play.

Parents should support and stand by teachers who are completely devoted to the vocation, and take care so teachers are rewarded for their tiring tasks. If it happens that your child does not bring home satisfactory marks for studying, then search for the reasons. Do not allow a teacher to be accused that he or she is incompetent and cannot create wise people from the ignorant ones without an investigation.

---

[64] *unexamined or unreflective*

Sexual Life

Life during today's time is at best pathological, which all the preceding chapters already point out. Bodily organs for increasing the species are getting weaker. But on what else depends the health and happiness of future generations? Today more than ever before it is necessary to point out that our duty is to not only preserve our health, but also to promote universal, scientific knowledge. It is not presently within the reach of the common woman of our countryside, and that is not because of the price of books, but of the comprehension required of the book's contents.

Lack of education here causes the majority of the written word to not be understood. And that these scientific books we and others do not understand, is not so much our fault as it is the fault of circumstances.

Many times I have mused about how the suffering of poor women could be lightened and how it could be accomplished that they would comprehend or try to understand, and thus lighten a mother's task and defend her womanliness in the presence of her husband's coarseness. Over and over I came to the same point - subject - and that is namely that women themselves must raise themselves from wailing and suffering, enforce the respect for the laws of nature, and observe health rules.

On the sex life, it was looked on always as something depraved. Coarse, mere fulfilled passions, and the woman gender was forced to yield, which is not humane. That is what was happening among common people, and I presume that even among the wealthy class of people it was not any better, because divorce meets divorce, and the wealthy wives fill the waiting rooms of doctors the same as the class of poor people. And this is a sad sight of mankind.

Much indeed, much rests in the hands of women, and that is because they can and should conduct the education of youth. An improved future for women rests in the hands of women - mothers, wives, and teachers. Therefore, please, for everything that is dear to you, think this over seriously what I want to tell you. I will tell you everything that I have observed on myself and on others - this is a serious subject.

Realize that we live here only once, and with the kind of life which we ourselves prepare. Remember that truth and reality are genuine, and truth never can stand to be ridiculed, even though sometimes it must struggle very hard. And false shyness gives rise to as much woe and unhappiness as coarse ignorance. About what now I want to converse is exactly that about which people are taught - not to directly speak the truth, or avoid it, but privately to misuse, and be like animals. And after all, this truth - the origin of every human - is fact before which some shut their eyes and others fight over: sex life means continuation of human species - thus it should be looked on as something holy, as something magnificent. If we ourselves make it vulgar, we are fakes, and are ashamed of ourselves. The first, and also second, are immensely stupid and worthy of reprimand.

Consider that every wise landlord examines the soil; he attempts to become acquainted with its characteristics and requirements. He examines and scrutinizes the seeds he sows; he observes his domesticated animals, and so forth. Equally any man of any type of craft studies, examines, and tries to discern the fundamental characteristics to turn to advantage all instruments. Whoever does not do this is either a person spiritless or rather a careless fellow, to put it briefly, a person who is deserving of his failures.

But what does an ordinary person know about his reproductive organs and laws of nature and rules of health? Nothing! The more educated people should know more - but do they? Our mankind and her afflictions indicate that they do not care to know! However, I cannot resist giving the truth and observations I have acquired, to the people who may be longing for the knowledge.

There is a sizable difference between the body of a man and a woman, where the work muscles, bodily perseverance, patience and other things are concerned. Man is here for the reason to impregnate, to protect his reproductive organs, and to preserve life.

The woman again is here to bear the man's seed, nurture it, and to prepare it for life. For this function, according to gender, the bodily organs are formed. How these organs appear is not necessary to write about. The inner constitution would be impossible to describe here without accurate illustrations.

Astonishing is that the organs of a man and woman, apparently different, really in their formation, are alike. About three months after conception, according to doctors, the fetus begins to show the gender, and in four months it is possible to ascertain undeniably the gender of the being, of course, only by dissection, post mortem examination.

According to my own and other women's belief and conviction, parents can select the gender. For this reason, as a matter of fact, I decided to let my experiences be written and printed out. Not ten times, but several hundred times I read or heard how unhappy parents were and still are unhappy because they did not have, and do not produce, children of both sexes.

Famous is the case of the last Russian Czarina who bore only daughters. The promise of her court doctors that the name of the one who advises her will be immortal, and that even a reward for advice will be paid in gold - all this impelled me to disclose what I know, that it is possible to predict gender. Parents can have their wish, a son or daughter, if they conduct themselves according to certain rules.

According to my theory, the man's seed is without gender. Instead, the woman's organ has the beginnings of both sexes, and the ovary on the left side has the male embryo. Up until now, sexual position was determined by chance, without understanding of the performance of inner organs of the childbearing mother. Until now the act was subordination and not wise reflection, therefore no one knew. However, I myself recognized that there are rules, and those we must follow, and we will always have a satisfactory result regarding the selection of gender.

Doctors were unable to believe me, or rather did not want to, and therefore it is necessary to write about the inner organs of a woman, so as to understand why the rules during contact must be observed, so the resulting gender would be the one expected.

It seems that parents who have children only of one gender, always performed the act of intercourse in the same bodily position. To this it is fitting to mention, that I observed that the mother who bore only one gender, suffered more ill health, pain in the bodice, legs, and womb - why so?

After further reflection, I came to the conclusion that the procreative organs[65] do not work alternately. Besides that, the husband, of course unaware, even tormented his despairing child bearer, because she did not bear him a son or daughter. This type of behavior has the consequence that it completely undermines the wife's health. And who is the cause of this lack of success? Neither of the couple because here null is their will, but *chance* mostly determines the sex.

The woman's organs, it is true, have only one entrance, but in the most back part it is divided into two equally important ovaries - small and strawberry-like. They are in both sides of the womb in a wide ligament somewhat attached, but with no passage connected; behind this, from the womb, two tubes lead to each ovary - one to each ovary. From these two[66] tubes the ovaries protrude and disperse and they resemble a flower.

This dispersion during a woman's menstrual period attaches to the ovary and from there eggs are produced, as the doctors claim. Each of these eggs, if filled with cells as science says, these cells in each ovary contain about 36,000 eggs. To the bare human eye they are invisible, only under a microscope is it possible to see their presence.

---

[65] *Marie is referring to the ovaries*
[66] *fallopian*

These cells are ripe during the menstrual period. Then they burst and release an egg, which is invisible to the naked eye, and its circumference is an insignificantly small figure - 0.1 or 0.2 millimeters in size. According to doctors, this egg is maybe even divided, and with tassels or dispersion are caught by the tube or egg tunnel with the aid of its own muscles that are continually in motion, is led down into the womb. Here they are fertilized if given the opportunity; if not, then they are led away by the menstrual flow.

Doctors claim that it is pure chance which gender a being will be when borne into this world. Gender supposedly no one is able to predict. Scientifically it is proven that no food, nourishment, no will, or stronger inclination of the woman or the man toward cohabitation brings about a child of the gender wished by the parents. This then is the doctor's theory, and further nothing is known.

I, however, as mentioned earlier, claim that it is possible to preselect gender. I believe that up until now, here the main role was played by chance, because parents did not know how to bring an heir into the world of the gender that they desired. Here it is necessary that the parents are really aware of what they want, so that they live prudently, and not deliberately work against nature.

A human being is endowed with intellect, and according to this should conduct self. Even the most ignorant animal better observes the rules of nature. It only occasionally gratifies its impulses, but a human does so as many times as he fancies. Everything on earth has its place, its purpose - even the seed in the life of a human.

I maintain that decent, prudent parents are able to bear not only healthy, beautiful, wise children, but also, children of the gender they desire. The ovary on the right side of the mother is the emissary of the female gender, and the ovary on the left of the womb of the mother is the male emissary.

It is known that during contact of man and woman, not only the sheath, but also the female receptacle - the womb - moves involuntarily. The male's seed is transported inside the moving sheath into the neck of the womb and then is suctioned into the womb. This motion is initiated by the arousal of the bearing organs, and is the same sensation that is elicited by the male's arousal and satiation of his procreative instincts. Well, then, man's life-giving embryo is suctioned into the mother's interior and there it meets the egg, fertilizes it, and by chance the sex is either male or female. This then is left up to chance - but it need not be.

However, I do not intend to argue with doctors about this that they call "ovary" because they have instruments and opportunities to research these life-giving mysteries. However, I remind you simply that doctors with all their knowledge, to this day cannot confirm the reason for monthly menses, nor can they precisely write about the mysterious origin of the gender in the mother's organs. About this I cannot tell the doctors more than I have observed and tested on others and myself. Not only this, but I was ambitious, and experimented and observed animal mothers.

The most interesting observation of these animal mothers is there are cases where they bear young of both sexes at one time. There it is possible to clearly see that a particular side / ovary brings a particular gender. The human mother bears usually one child, but if more are born then interesting is my theory. The strongest support is this - that sometimes there are twins born conjoined, but these Siamese were never male and female genders, but always either both male or both female and never one of each sex. Is this not sufficient for doctors to pay a little attention to my theory?

For my advice to this day many mothers and fathers are grateful. In my experience are found cases where married couples were endowed only with daughters; annoyed parents were seeking advice and help. Here was an opportunity to point to the regulations with which I became acquainted and behold, they had a son.

Elsewhere another couple had only boys - they did not believe me and had a son again. The mother sadly decided for strict obedience and obeyed my advice. She became impregnated and fearfully awaited the outcome. This was happy as a healthy girl was born. I can boldly say that out of ten cases, eight ended always the way I advised.

When a son is desired, the husband must take care that he is towards the wife's left side during intercourse. In the important interval when on the back, he must not forget his goal, because it is necessary that he lie back to her left side, and she turns to him. With this move she is on her left side and he on his right. In this instant is decided the gender of the child.

I do not believe that fertilization of the egg by the man's semen takes more than five minutes. In doctors' books one reads that the man's egg is in the womb even eight days, and that anywhere during this time the egg could be fertilized. If the seed enters the ovary by accident it does not get fertilized, but a growth called a "tumor" grows which then must be removed by operation.

Therefore, it is good to make the act as short as possible in order to avoid various miscreations[67]. If the act is of long duration and the woman lies on the back, then the man's seed may enter the bottom of the womb and both ovaries work, and usually it happens that both sexes are born.

If my theory is correct, then parents must observe the direction as I have written them. If the desired gender is not achieved, this could be because the woman was not impregnated the first time or even the second, so then the third attempt the parents may have disregarded my directions and the woman was impregnated - perhaps even after the sixth attempt or so - when neither bothered to follow my directives.

---

[67] *e.g., tumors*

As I introduced previously, the fertilization act is equal to the most magnificent function of which man is capable. That is because two people, without asking the potential child, bring him into this world. This act should be regarded as something godlike. This ought to be instilled into the young people's minds, where the parents or teachers observe that life drives are beginning to make demands. And then we would not have on earth immoral people, and people with physical impairments.

Therefore, parents should not call into this world their descendents thoughtlessly. If they want this responsibility, let them think it over well, and conceive children who will be lively, witty, and who will live according to the laws of nature. When they want a son, let them create a son, and if a daughter, then observe the regulations opposite of the ones in the first case. Then the husband lies on his left side and she on her right.

If the parents are able to feed and educate more children, then they should alternate the genders because the mother does not suffer as much because the organs work alternately. Her body does not suffer as much, and annoyance and unjust accusations that the husband is ruining her health are avoided beforehand.

It is necessary that after every act the wife remain on her side not less than five minutes. Perhaps it will be even better if she remains so longer. It is possible that the man's seed adheres to the egg sooner - maybe it is enough only the turn of the body during the act, but certainty is certainty. The rules should be kept until the partners feel sure that the wife is impregnated.

Well then, this is what from my experiences and those of others I have revealed. In others rests the task to examine and search further. I remind you once more, that it is necessary to follow the advice exactly, if the parents are really serious about selecting the gender of the newborn. Even a small variation or omission before actual conception can reverse the wish of the parents. Many have testified to me that this is true. Where I was asked for advice, the desired gender was achieved in eight out of ten cases.

Why it was not achieved in some cases is hard to tell. Perhaps because a husband forgot to obey, because one doubted the theory, and perhaps another was lax. When some couples had only children of one gender, finally they obeyed my advice - the result? They had the gender desired. Then the husband laughed no more and the wife was grateful that she found out the truth about my theory which both doubted previously. And after all, it is not so unbelievable, when we know that everything in this world has its rules, which it is necessary to observe and follow if we want to obtain success. Well then, this should suffice, isn't that so? As to the logic of my theory, for what other reason would a woman's inside be divided? If both ovaries contained material for both genders, wouldn't one ovary suffice?

I am remembering how once a father of four little girls came to me, referred by a friend who had long ago called children into the world. And the friend told the father that I advised him well and that I would also advise the friend well. It happened that they had a fifth daughter. I kindly chided him, and told his sister to advise her woeful sister-in-law. Not even a year went by and they had a son. Then the father did not know what to do from JOY. Maybe now there will be more young Thomas children.

Sad was the case, when a man wished to have a son and did not get one. The mother, shivering with fear to his question as to what gender was born said, "A daughter." He, blinded by rage, flung the child, which died immediately. The mother, still tortured with pain, fainted. Where here in this type of case is the ability to reason? Where, when in this type of heavy hour he loses all consideration, and suddenly ruins his good wife, child, and the whole family?

Another case was that in a certain family they had two little girls, and the mother suffered after each birth. She desired a son, and when she saw that the husband had the same wish, she would gladly undergo new pain, if only their wishes could be fulfilled. I advised her. Distrustfully she looked at me and we spoke no more. A while later we met again, and seeing that she was expecting, I asked her some questions, as is the right of older women. After her answers I said to her, "My dear girl, you will again have a girl."

She, surprised, asked how could I know that? "From experience, from experience!" I answered. Another year passed, they followed my advice, and the next time a boy was born. There was joy and gaiety. Once, when I visited there when the boy was already walking, the happy father, giving me his hand as a welcome, was happily showing me the boy, saying, "Look - my son. How happy it will be in this world later, when it is known everywhere how to call a boy or girl into this world!"

Some married couples in gratitude gave me a notarized paper as proof my theory worked, and many from false modesty refused to give me a confirmation, although there was a time when I asked for one only to prove to doctors my theory is correct.

A certain lady was longing for a daughter, but to me she did not confide. After a time, she came after me, and showing her little girl, said, "If there would not have been this little one, I would not believe you. But now I know that what you know is the real truth. (One of the mothers who used my advice had informed her.) According to this, I judge that my knowledge is beginning to spread among people. I wish everyone happiness, luck, and contentment.

About Preventing Conception

Some wives/mothers who have birthed more than once yield with fear[68] to the husband's touch, and whenever they can, they avoid the meeting. Today, when people understand and reflect about human life, when they are certain that a person cannot support self, few others will support them. Thus, with apprehension and worry they are expecting a fifth or sixth addition into the family. This worry and anxiety of course has a much stronger effect on the mother than the father - wives usually are more sensitive than men. Fears and then economical social conditions force women to perform various heavy work, for which their bodies were not created - as a result the female gradually bears more and more children and in successively greater pain.

Mankind's arrival into this world not at all originally signified pain, but today it is a torture. Still this woman in travail is happy if she has a good and compassionate husband. It is worse for the woman whose husband has no pity - never a kind word, and he does not allow her any rest. If all the men would be perceptive enough, then the ones whose wife died as a result of bodily weakening would be placed into a house of correction built for this purpose. They would not deserve anything else. It is a blot on the husband's character when the wife has to be operated on due to the weakening of her childbearing organs. The various bumps, tumors, and cancers exist because the law of nature was overstepped. In today's times, wives are terribly punished with these defects, but it is not their fault but the husbands'. As I observed, merely two times out of ten does a woman suffer through her own wrongdoing. Today, when a man's wife dies he is pitied, and according to supportive customs of friends, they soon are fretting that he should quickly remarry.

For every transgression of the laws of nature, there is a punishment. For every injury on the body of one's fellow creature, we are punished with a fine or prison; in fact, people who kill their opponents in a fight are closed in the prison or sentenced to death. But when a man misuses his rights toward his weak wife, when he

---

[68] *of impregnation*

forces her, against her will, to bear - insists that she gratify his every whim - for that there is no punishment. How glad and happy I would be if I would have the gift of ability to convince all men how inhumanly the guilty ones are acting in this regard.

How much unjust suffering thousands of women undergo, and only because they are women. The woman-mother who undergoes this kind of callousness, she is regarded lower than any other form of animal by such husbands. It is a stigma that man, the king of creatures, is the only creature on earth that is often unable or unwilling to observe the compassionate laws of nature.

Healthful satiation of their instincts does not signify sickness or suffering, but delight from which spins not only new life, but also desire for useful work. And as I previously remarked, immediately during their youth, people ought to be taught that the purpose of marriage is the union of two different sexes to fulfill a task magnificent, a task god-like, and that people should not look to this union as the satiation of their impure impulses.

If only people would be taught during their youth and led to the understanding that man will never be happy, and cannot be so until he fulfills his obligations toward his fellow creature - then so many children would not be born. People would reflect, and control themselves. Today, woe to the wife who will not submit. Not only because the man would tyrannize her, but the world would condemn her. "I want," is valid for the man, and, "I have to," is expected for the woman. That is why so many women fall into a premature grave.

If the men would attempt self-control, and fill their minds with purer thoughts, then their impulses would not torture them, and instead of being hated, their wives would love them. It is not true that a man must give in to his arbitrariness, or must for reason of health gratify himself. Nature knows how to forestall man's organ overfilling without the man's body suffering. But when once these organs are roused, then of course bad effect presents itself if they are not satiated.

Therefore men should be aware that they should not unnecessarily be sexually aroused, guard themselves from impure thoughts, avoid undignified thoughts, and if they are so fragile that the mere presence of a loving wife rouses and tempts them into recklessness, then they should conduct themselves sensibly, and not unnecessarily injure their wives' bodies. If the wife is willing to submit to his passion, or if she has to, let him not vex her with force. Also, a man has no right to accuse his wife or even torture her because she again was impregnated. A man should have sense! He, after all, knows and has more opportunities to inform and educate himself than does a woman who is working all day for the family. Let men remember this and act accordingly.

But I know that this booklet will also be read by men who will not want to harm their brides and don't intend to. These men possess the intelligence to recognize and understand the purpose of life, and also the social relations. For these kind of considerate and sensible men my preaching does not concern, but maybe I can be of benefit to the others, and so I am gladly doing this.

Many men in order to relieve their bride and not hurt her, deny themselves their sexual desire to their own detriment, and as a result they suffer. A loving wife, seeing this, torments herself too, and both become unhappy. Is this necessary? No - when they know how to restrict the results of the act of cohabitation.

Young people cannot help it that they must love. Love is the purpose, with whose help nature not only preserves, but also enables continuation of the human race from time immemorial. The reason the act of intercourse was chosen for procreation is unknown to us, but is necessary. If there would be no intercourse, people could maybe grow even on willows. And lovemaking is not only a right of life but also its destiny.

Therefore, no one has the right to restrain pure and moral conduct of two people who sincerely like each other and long for each other. If they are restrained due to religion or perhaps narrow-mindedness, the couple is tempted very often into sexual impropriety. This leads to, as competent judges claim, illness of both. In women illness occurs when they feel the need to appease sexual instincts and are not satisfied. The effects are no less harmful than the results in other women of giving birth too frequently. Both are transgressions against nature.

For these types of cases doctors try to think of means by which impregnation could be avoided. When the man requests appeasing and the woman does not feel this need, then even without help impregnation can easily be prevented with this: that the seed is not sown. Think it over! The seed is not sown but at the same time the instinct is appeased outwardly. But when both desire and the act is interrupted before the wife reaches satisfaction, then her health suffers.

This does not happen otherwise in the husband. Therefore doctors condemn and reprimand these persons who commit this. The result of this action is no different on one's health as self-abuse and is a scourge of mankind. Young people, in consideration of how to prevent enlargement of the family, in an unnatural manner tire their bodies. They call out sexual desire, but the well being of health they cannot substitute. From this rises bad temper, irritation, and drain on vital strength. The result is digestive disturbance in men, exhaustion and diseased organs in women. The most blissful marriage becomes unhappy, and a rigid bond of two lovers is loosened.

This occurs everywhere where a couple is not morally strong enough to be able to suppress in themselves that which, as a matter of fact, a person is obliged to perform if he does not want his kind to disappear from the face of the earth. Therefore we do not have the right to damn two people who love each other, that they are erring when they cannot resist their instincts, but a large family they cannot have and do not want. For when their sexual instinct in a natural and honorable manner makes itself known, a person must not be reprimanded and belittled.

However, those who exchange it for passion or with drinking of alcohol, or as a matter of fact, for this purpose with selected food stimulates it and in an unnatural way appeases it, he is worse than an animal and deserves punishment. That kind deals improperly with sexual instinct and in an undignified manner.

Well, then, if a man does not wish to impregnate his wife he does not have to, if at the crucial moment the spurt of the seed is led elsewhere. However, this method to many is against the modesty and refined mind of the wife. But there where both long for the closeness of their bond although they fear the results and they cannot perform their family duty, there exactly for the above reasons it is impossible to recommend this method. Here it is necessary to know that during amorous excitement of a man and woman - organs are filled with blood and nerves are excited to a convulsive poignancy, and excited muscles, after natural appeasement, again are calmed.

During interruption of the act, the man maybe reaches his peak and is calmed in the correct manner. Not so the wife. Here turns up the damage, and if the act is repeated with inappropriate finish, the woman is taken ill and although her body was not damaged by too many childbirths, her body is damaged here just the same. This is a condemnation-worthy manner of sexual intercourse. This results in more births of children with impairments, and in the end this is due to the husband's carelessness about the process of woman's impregnation. Then not only both suffer but also the child.

Those who are familiar with life, especially the life of poor people - the torment of women in agriculture, the labor, their difficult child-bearings, poverty, their want of everything, that hurry - do not be surprised that those knowledgeable do not tell everyone what they know about how to prevent conception. Every one of you knows about need, sickness, and the like. How glad every one of us is when we learn of some help, and when one can escape these sufferings.

Doctors do advise the wealthy, because long ago doctors learned how to avoid large families. Only the uneducated must multiply like rabbits. Yet, in the wars, like the rabbit they pursue them - the poor - to be soldiers, and like the rabbit they kill them. We are people like the wealthy lords in that we already have various means to prevent conception. And the main method is abstinence. This is, however, not ideal for young persons. No one is born who doesn't have these sexual instincts unless they are bodily unable or if their strength is corroded by disease.

A moral person, even though he is forced by life to have concern about his agriculture and thus needs help with the work[69], if he does not desire to enlarge his family, or to harm the wife, here will be presented additional knowledge to prevent conception.

Before I point them out, I again claim that a healthy young couple is obliged to give the world children. The saddest attitude of a couple is that children are a burden. There let both realize that they are not thinking correctly when they desire to satisfy their sexual instinct without fulfilling the obligation to the world to procreate and thus to contribute to the world - the past, present, and future. There the married couple acts improperly and their punishment will be that one day they will realize that their health, their peace, and contentedness they ruined for themselves.

But when we once find out how to avoid conception, then the march of our thought must not be stopped, else it is not possible to benefit from the knowledge of how to avoid it - unnecessary duty placed on us by life. Remember that there are many aids in our distress, unpleasant restraints resulting in sad circumstances aroused from the lack of knowledge of man.

The world is not overpopulated. Much time it would take until the people would have nothing to eat. How much work here on earth would need to be done before the world would be changed into the Garden of Eden! Ignorance drags on every step of progress and also on science, but if I may triumph over ignorance, this triumph gives the world a procedure how to avoid conception.

These procedures are varied and the doctors have already spent their time developing them in the recent past. They are utilized, of course, for the wealthy the most often. Some of these methods are

---

[69] *and has children to assist him with the agriculture work*

designed for men but are available mostly to women. These various methods ought to and should serve merely to assure that the woman who already bore would be protected and children already born would not have to be pushed aside and short-changed. These methods should protect health and family harmony. Each one of these methods has the goal to prevent the entrance of the man's seed into the womb.

Many chemicals were discovered which kill the seed. Also there was designed a cover for the male organ made from the rubber substance of a fish's bladder. These condoms are obtainable in pharmacies. However, this purveyance is said to be for many unpleasant, and some men say that it incites nervous disorders. Sometimes they even tear, and, for this reason, they are not exactly a reliable help. Besides this, it is said men do not like to make themselves inconvenienced, especially those who are without consideration nor care regarding what will result later due to their indolence.

On the other side there are many means intended for women. But women's organs are not all alike, and for this reason every woman cannot with certainty use them without practice. One device is called a "diaphragm" and it should sit on the cervix. But in women who have given birth often, the diaphragm cannot close the opening.

The most common method, which all women can use, is a piece of doctor's cotton or wadding, but a clean small cloth is better. I repeat, however, a *clean* small cloth. The cloth or wadding before using is soaked in a solution of vinegar water. The solution has the function of destroying the man's seed. The cloth must be so placed as to cover the opening to the womb, and thus prevent the seed from entering. The edge of the cloth should be tied to a thread so that later it could be taken out.

Another method is rinsing out the organ, but it must be done immediately after the act. This is not a reliable nor comfortable method. For this is needed a syringe, and the water should be warm with an addition of vinegar. Cold water must not be used, or else the woman will become ill. This I point out emphatically.

Yet another procedure is the so-called "protective ring" – the invention of Dr. Caves. This, when set on the cervix, and if placed so that it can be filled with a "borovou" [*a Czech word meaning "solution made from a pine, or Scotch fir tree"*] which destroys the seed. The solution slowly radiates from the ring and spills on the tip and surroundings. It has the advantage that it does not interrupt, and it is not necessary to remove it often or replace it before every act. They say it is very popular as it does not offend the sensibilities or decency and is not detrimental. Also used is a special sprayer. These methods are fairly expensive and hard to obtain.

Besides those named, there are still several other types of assists but it seems they are not as popular as the ones previously named. For all, except using the small cloth, a doctor must advise, which is to many women a detriment. It is necessary here that every woman knows herself what her organ shape needs to avoid conception. I point out that if the kind of protection used during the act is disturbing, and does not give gratification, then the couple does not live contentedly even though acting frugally.

In such a case they must find a procedure that will satisfy both. Towards contributing to the contentment of loving moral people, I can boldly say that people who are summoned to this calling should consider how they can help others. Before this book is read it may be that there will be invented a method without faults that will be a blessing for all when they have a family and do not want more, or are unable to do so.

False prophets claim that destroying human seed is a sin. However, a sensible person will agree that a much greater sin is to bring children into the world and then let them be knocked around in the world. Each seed in nature (plant or animal) is composed of the same material and all look alike. All then mean the continuation of life and all are unending eternity after which flow ages and unknown future.

But look how much plant seed in the world is ruined or unutilized by nature! This unused seed, even the largest measure or estimate amounts to a figure for which a human word is inadequate. How much of the available plant seed is used for the livelihood of man and animal? And how much comes to ruin while sowing - how much has to be chopped out? But that waste is *not* a sin?

I know many cases where it would be better to ruin the seed rather than the ripe fruit. I will point to only one case. In a certain parish lives a couple, and after a time of 13 years, they already have 10 children. What type of care can these parents in these situations give these children? Especially if they are poor tenants like these.

The father's earnings alone are inadequate for the sustenance of the family, and so the wife helps. But that isn't all. So that suffering would be overflowing, the last two children were twins, as can often happen in such families. She becomes ill. A doctor is needed. No one knew what the mother needed because organic faults on her were not detected.

When she unhappily complained, I told her in plain terms: "What is the matter with you? It is that you are exhausted, overworked with fieldwork, weakened by childbearing and inadequate diet - you're rushing to your grave. The best medicine for you is if your husband gives you peace, hires help for the fields, and gives you plenty of nourishing food, and then you will be healthy!"

Will she receive this? Hardly. People are so unaware that they are unable to figure out that the bad luck comes cheaper. From the 10 children some already died. Due to inadequate care, one child lay in bed. Little bones protruded through the flesh and it pitifully perished.

It is no wonder that we meet in our life with these woeful events. What good then can come from this type of cohabitation to which a woman is forced against her will? Improving a bad personality later is impossible when the bad foundation was laid at its beginning.

For your own good, husbands, stop and do not seek your wife when you yourself feel wretched. When you are angry beware to embrace, from which might emerge a third. If a child is born to you whom you gave the foundation of an impairment, which happens to children of alcoholics, no professor can make a philosopher out of him. If you produce an impaired person, all the doctors in the world are unable to make a healthy youth out of him.

Therefore I beg all of you to stop and think and ponder before you take the step to call forth a third person. Indeed, to be sure, it is a great responsibility.

From My Experiences

During the passage of years, when I waited upon and advised women, I pondered various thoughts and went through many cases, which always presented occasion for new conjectures. Several times with new evidence was presented a proof that on an old opinion can be built an invulnerable fact.

I observed a child's nature, character, and during my services to child-bearing women I gave attention to the time of the year when the child was born, and I searched for the time when his life was given a beginning, and I came upon a surprising conclusion. These experiences I will share with you and I wish that people would think about them and examine them. I believe it is the duty of people to elevate their race, to preserve and extend it.

There is no person on earth who, when he wants to become a father or mother, would not wish for himself children who are intelligent, and pretty or handsome. We know well, that the lame would like to walk, but cannot for his inadequacy. The blind would like to see, but is unable because he has no vision; and similarly it is with all human faults. If a person is endowed with various abilities, it is not due to his merit, just as it is not a fault of a mentally challenged person that they did not bring into this world a godly gift.

Once long ago I read that it was verified by an operation that all the scholars, the great thinkers, had their brain covered with a particular gray matter, and this was the phenomenon of their great capability. It further stated there that if a person has a brain covered with a dark membrane, he is incapable of a single thought at all. At the end of this article, there were introduced a few words stating that it would be of great value if parents would know what foundation to give a child so that desirable traits would be brought into the world. This remark stuck in my memory, and many times at night, instead of sleep, I entertained myself with this thought. I suppose that parents too should cohabit only when they can control themselves. Utilizing brains and self-control have never harmed anyone yet.

We all know well that when the weather is beautiful, and bright, and air is clean, that one and all of us feel cheerful. If it is gloomy, foggy, or sultry, a person feels accordingly. This even influences the origin of the child. With one certain case my opinion I confirm. I remind couples not to conceive their child on a gloomy or stormy day. I must mention that other women who were able to recall on the happening in their life agreed with me. Certainly, everyone knows industrious children. And surely everyone is acquainted with a lazy fellow, an idler.

Have you several times thought that it would be best to avert creating this type of people in this world? I believe that even in this, parents could accomplish much. Parents before cohabitation ought to occupy themselves with some type of pleasant work, or talk about it with the intention that they will do this. If the wealthy would do this, surely their children would not suffer with boredom, as from birth their brain would not allow them to be lazy. This I firmly believe, that laziness comes from the type of people who only think of sleep, good eating, and drinking. Children conceived during this kind of parental mood are lazy and selfish.

I see in life all types of people, and many of them are very morose, surly persons. They have no pleasure in anything. And although they work hard and are thrifty, something always gets in their way, and what they made turns into nothing. Here I presume that the child was called into this world during a moment when the parents themselves were feeling unhappy.

In order to ensure that a child will be happy and have success in everything, conceive him at the moment when you both feel happy. Every builder, who wishes to build a good pretty home, in the first place sees to it that he obtains strong materials. He thinks it over and makes sketches before he begins building. He hires conscientious, honest workers, and oversees cautiously the whole building. His pride will be the pretty and long-lasting, durable house.

How much more important is a father's mission. It is sad to think that today most persons indulge the impulses of their bodies, which affect the human race, without regard for immortality. Unscrupulous people do not sow seeds for eternity, or even receive them with the right awareness. They squander them, degrade themselves, and originate unhappy blossoms. And this happens merely from imprudence and ignorance.

Many believe in the Lord of the world, others in a godly person, a Deity, but all belittle the highest degree of their own strength and make their descendents unhappy. We call this strength, but the truth remains that people of their own free will misuse and undervalue their seed of immortality. Many do not use procreation for the improvement of their descendents, but to satisfy their lusts and pleasures. That is the greatest sin that people commit.

Each one of you probably knows of a case where a child is borne into this world as a physically challenged person. Parents previously had children who were healthy and strong. All of a sudden the mother bears a physically challenged child - small hands and feet maimed, harelips, without fingers, or fingers joined together, etc. This mutilation is not the child's fault, but perhaps the parents committed transgressions against nature.[70] Maybe the father or mother are not the cause directly, but transgression was committed by the grandfather, grandmother, or even still farther back.

It is not said in vain that the sinner's descendents are punished to the fourth generation. Old sins cannot be made up for any other way except careful abiding of the laws of nature. If it so happens that a stain, or defect, appears because of transgressions in past generations, then our conscience is clear and the blow of fate is borne more easily.

---

[70] *here again the reader is reminded to consider the limits of knowledge regarding the effects of nature vs. nurture (e.g., DNA, heredity versus modeled behavior) during Marie's era*

The saddest fact of today's upbringing is this kind of case, and it is not isolated: a girl comes to school for a textbook and mentions that she is getting married! What does she know? What does she understand? Nothing! She does not know how to wash clothes, cook food. She does not know what economizing is. Indeed she does not know as much as during my time a twelve-year-old knew about housework. And if two such young people do not run away from each other after a few Sundays or weeks, before the year meets with another year then they will say good-bye when they have a descendent. If they can bear staying together for six years, then there are four descendents. And then one wonders where poverty comes from.

Yes, I believe this firmly, that parents with their mind and thought can influence the child during procreation, and then the mother for the whole time of its development can influence the fruit of her womb. Again, this I point out, that women in the impregnated condition beware and avoid various desires and lusts, especially those that are detrimental to health. That old wives' tale that a pregnant woman must have everything she thinks of is very harmful and wrong. It does no harm to the woman that she cannot get what she would like, but being upset that she cannot have it is harmful to her. A woman who is greedy and selfish, transfers these characteristics to the developing child, and this way they twist a broom on themselves. If the father of the child is no better, then no one can be surprised that there are so many spoiled children.

I believe too that the sun also has a great effect on the human being, and affects the brain. The moon effects the human being's age, and various constellations have various effects on the efficiency and health of a human. If people would understand, they could avoid all types of unpleasantness for themselves, and also perfect and improve their children's bodies and mentalities.

Long ago, people could conceive that from one set of parents came forth children maybe in the amount of 12, and seldom does it happen that two look exactly alike, or that they have the same nature and inclination to work on studies. To this realization I have rich experiences. There was one case where a married couple, people honorable and wealthy, had three sons. As soon as the boys finished the community school, they were sent off to study. One of the boys became a priest, the second a judge, and the third a regular scoundrel. Once this scoundrel, after many wanderings, came to a place where his brother served as a parish parson. He came to the rectory where his brother welcomed him pleasantly, fed him, bought him a new suit, and gave him money. He took it all with thanks. He put on the clothes, but almost as soon as he came out of the rectory, he took off the clothes and sold them, then went to the tavern and there spent all the money on liquor. From the village he left again like a ragamuffin.

Once I was working in a mill for a very respected, esteemed family. At 11 o'clock one night, someone was knocking at the door. I went there and asked, "Who's that?" "The miller's son," a voice answered, "Let me in." I opened the door and into it pushed a low-down looking man, a knotty stick in his hand, barefooted, and he pushed himself into the room. I became frightened and called the housewife and told her that he had said that he was the miller's son. The lady of the house then reprimanded me because I had let him in. I defended myself – that he said he was the miller's son. They let him sleep there, but in the morning one could say they chased him away. Then for a long time they were afraid that he might retaliate and burn their property. This was puzzling and mysterious to me, and I saw in this what type of people are in the world, and apparently, most likely, they cannot help what they do. There are various visible events which have a great influence on children, young people, and adults - especially those who are not firm enough to resist evil. If then their nature pulls them down, then soon they will fall. Because of this, people should be mindful before they call upon a new person to enter the world.

Elsewhere I again became acquainted with a married pair who had four children - a girl and three boys. The girl was severely impaired. The physician said to bathe her in herb bath water so her tiny swollen body would lose its unnatural largeness and also its life. The mother did this several times, but then, after all, compassion did not allow her to continue. Love was stronger and the love asked that the child live. She ceased to bathe her and was consoling herself that maybe the child would outgrow it. She did not grow out of it, and the parents had to feed her and clean her. If she started crying there was no stopping her, and if she laughed, her laughter had no end. The doctor did an autopsy on one of her brothers after death, and instead of a brain, the boy had a cavity filled with water. Another son grew to adulthood, but at first the girls were afraid to go with him as his children might bring into the world the same faults as his brothers and sister. However, his children were healthy and beautiful.

Another married couple had the first child healthy, nicely grown. After him, a heartrending child who was crippled was born. The little hands and feet were mutilated and strewn with bumps. The mother was desperate. I did not soothe her because it would have been dishonest. On the contrary, I told her, "The child will not grow and probably will not live ten years, maybe five." As destiny would have it for the mother, the child died in five months.

To a certain married couple a child was born. The top half of the body was regularly developed. But the lower part resembled a fish. Another time another child was born with a normal body, but the little face was shaped like a frog.

Here observing carefully the day of birth, and tracing the development at origin, I came upon the thought that the origin was always definitely on an unfavorable day. If there is an interest in this work of mine, later I will offer what I observed in that direction, which led me to a certain woman, who observes nature and its influence on life from a diverse standpoint.

It is a certainty, that everything is influenced by other forces, but it seems to me that at the end there lingers human intellect. In every instance it is better if human intellect and firm will overrules, rather than expect science and fine arts to repair whatever damage man caused when he erred either from ignorance or ill-will.

A particular mother once bore a child who had no roof in the mouth. The distraught parents went from doctor to doctor. $600 they paid out for its cure, and it helped nothing. The child died uncured. What was the use of all the worries and pains of childbirth, the expense and sorrow, when everything they tried appeared to the poor parents to be a huge zero. What a contrast was another married pair who had 6 children - 4 sons and 2 daughters. All married and from this six pairs there are 19 people on earth. All are healthy, intelligent, and happy. Ancestors like this in the first generation did not indulge in their impulses insensibly, and the younger ancestors were even more moderate. On all their effort lay success. And these involve no witchcraft, no special luck. Intelligence reigns them and that is the magic and secret of the family.

Once when I was present at the birthing hour of a certain lady, there were several of us women there. As soon as the child was born, one of the ladies present bowed her head over the newborn and said, "A little girl! Ouch, again another slave came into the world!" This poor woman judged the child's fate according to her own. That time, a long time ago already it is, I thought to myself, "Oh, that you mothers would have the knowledge! Why do you not bear more boys, or equal numbers of genders?"

If the men would know that if their first wife dies, they will not get another one, surely they would regard their wives differently. It is certain that more women of a good nature die than those who are unpleasant. A unpleasant one will not get married because she is stubborn and will not yield. A good one is tormented and willfully destroyed.

At a certain occasion, I met with a certain lady whose husband had an occupation which demanded much thought. On a certain day he was especially in haste, but somehow cheered up and embraced his wife to himself, and she - too willingly - gave in. This sincere and affectionate moment, surrounded with a noble-minded thought, did not stand still without consequences. It appeared in the form of a little baby son. The child grew strong and healthy, and above all, on him was noticeable, remarkable diligence, and a tendency to do everything in the best way possible.

Once it happened that the lady forgot to make certain provisions for herself, and as chance would have it, she urgently needed this certain item. She sent the child to the neighbor to ask if she would be so kind as to loan her this item, and that she would return it soon. The little boy correctly relayed the message, and the mother went to town later and bought this item. The little boy incessantly reminded his mother of her obligation to return the borrowed item. This sense of obligation never left him, and to this day he is conscientious, punctual, and honest. He serves the public at large to satisfaction, and his family to good fortune. Perhaps then even you, Dear Readers, will remind yourself and reorient, and thus avoid much suffering with which today, in order to raise a child, one must struggle.

I am old today but you must admit that an older person should know all sorts of things, especially a person who has gone through a large section of the world, and who did not avert her eyes from anything, nor did she stop up her ears. Then this person already has a right to wisdom. The young know little because of their craftiness, and they forget about wisdom. Their liveliness will not allow them to think deeply - until they get rid of their wildness, until pain and worry they taste - then they become serious. And those are the ones who only now can realize peace and contentment. Because they admit that they were foolish, and that with intelligence no law of nature can be cheated.

What I wish is that these young ninnies would stop and read this catechism, that they would become absorbed in thought and reflect sometimes on the importance of human life on earth. To be sure, it becomes even young people to appear as people endowed with wisdom. And they are and will continue to renew human life on earth, and even they may come upon something new from which humanity may be improved. And even they can be an instrument capable of washing out a great deal of evil from the human race.

Perhaps even I myself may not see the good derived from them, for long ago my bones will have turned to dust. Yet even after I die, I will remain participating by my influence in their good deed of procreation in love, which will forever remain the method of conception of the living and the already dead. And this drive to love cannot do otherwise but continue to assert itself again for the living, for their joy and fortune. Yet everyone who acquires this book is asked not to leave it lying around so that it would fall into wrong hands – in no circumstances to children under 16 years of age. This I caution, because, I know humans well.

In many places, instead of good I could see evil. This book is written to instruct couples, and not children - who belong in school. The sacred duty of every mother is at an appropriate time to inform her descendents, but this she is obliged to do by words. A written word is not always clearly understood. Indeed, many adults are mentally so limited that they do not comprehend the most clearly disclosed truth – so how can a child?

The reasoning of a child develops progressively with the growth of the body. Even if the words are understood well, they cannot comprehend the meaning. And misunderstood ideas beyond their ability can lead them into an abyss. To guard against this is the parent's and instructor's duty, because if children become ne'er-do-wells, their lives will be poisoned because they did not receive proper, sincere instruction - and useless is crying later over ill fortune and bad fate.

Childbirth

It seems to me that this little booklet would be incomplete if I did not present something of my experiences which I collected among women during their difficult hour[71]. The first thing I can say is that a pregnant woman should have enough nourishment - but simple, unprocessed food - vegetables, light mealy food, and meat in the smallest amount possible, sweet milk or skim, and buttermilk according to appetite.

Hold on to this and do not create various dainty bits. The meat causes the fetus to strengthen its little head to grow and the child itself becomes fat, by which the birthing becomes heavy and painful. The meat causes the stools to be hard, and the temperature of the body is higher than it should be. So it is also with tea, strong coffee, and baked sweet goods.

Very often I think if children would be taught to be modest or discreet about their bodily symptoms, and if the mothers would teach them so, that they would come only to her with these symptoms and confide them to her, then there would not be so much impropriety and intemperance in people - it would not grow rampant. Everyone would be reluctant to admit publicly that through their own fault, or foolishness, or intemperance[72] they suffer, and that nature - like a mother - her disobedient child punishes with related symptoms.

The pregnant woman should have enough sleep, and the man should see to it that she has enough fruit so that during pregnancy nothing would bother her. He himself during this time should not excite her. The woman is herself to blame if she suffers extreme pain, as a result of the development of the child. It is better for the mother and two times better for the child if it is born thin but active. It, with correct diet, becomes strong faster and grows without difficulty.

---

[71] *childbirth*
[72] *e.g., lack of self-control regarding their diets*

Before the difficult hour should come, the mother should stand over hot water for at least a week, once a day. In the water may be boiled various herbs which make the childbirth easier and which calm the afterbirth pain.

If there are no herbs, water alone is adequate, above which the pregnant woman should stand and allow the steam to rise from the bottom of the body up to the top. She must take care that she does not get chilled or go into a draft of air.

As soon as she is through she may take some clean lard or oil and spread it on. As soon as the last hour comes it is very good to, with this lard, gently rub the chest beginning at the ribs on both sides. For this the helper must use both hands. I remind you that these helpers must not have sharp nails and must have clean hands because it could happen that through touch the woman in travail, or child, could be injured fatally. For the mother, of course, it is best when the painful hour is over as soon as possible. But I remind you that forcible help became fatal for many women.

If the helper is able, she knows if everything is going the natural way or not. To investigate this is easy, as the correct way of coming is that the little head shows itself first. The helper places her fingers into the womb and gently the top of the little head encircles. As soon as the mother is in pain, the helper gently presses again on the womb where the child's stomach is located.

In normal circumstances where the mother already knows her condition, and the household offers her everything that her condition demands, 98% of the children are born correctly, with the head first, and only 2 out of a 100 are born in a different way. If the birth is proceeding correctly, there is no need to help, but after each wave of pain when the mother wants to sleep, one must let her. During regular childbirth it is not necessary to help, because this is the work of nature and not something inappropriate. But where naturalness is absent, it is best to call a physician. Also, when the water breaks it is necessary to let a physician attend to it.

I know of a case where the mother could not give birth. We led her around for a while and then the child came head first, but as soon as she lay down, the child went back in. A doctor was called to help, but the child was injured and died after a short time. I will mention here the various directions so that you can advise one another during our heavy hours.

When the child comes, it is necessary for the health of the child and mother to let the mother take a good rest. We must realize that the child, up until now, lived in a constant temperature surrounded by fluid, was nourished by the mother's blood which brought it oxygenated blood filled with rich nourishment. Until the first suction of breath into little lungs, all necessary oxygen it received from the mother. The child has an average of 210 parts of blood but from that measure in its body it has about 60 parts. Most of it at this time is in the umbilical cord, and therefore it is not good to immediately separate it from the mother.

When the child all of a sudden finds itself outside in the cold and, to him, unpleasant atmosphere, his nerves as a result of the change begin to function and he begins to toss about, and thus his lungs begin to work. Oxygen, which up until now his mother with her blood provided, is not adequate for the development of the new body. The lungs at first widen, draw inside the first oxygen of air and this oxygen moves the blood, and thus the whole organism begins to function.

The naval cord should not be immediately tied, but wait about 10 minutes so that the lungs could have enough blood from the cord pumped into the new body. During a long-lasting labor, of course, it is necessary to behave otherwise, as the apparently lifeless body it is necessary to try to revive. Then the revived child, after about 10 minutes, is taken from the mother with a clean cloth, held a little further from the stomach, and still a little further tie the cord with clean cloth.

It is best first to pour hot water on the bandage before tying, and cut with sterilized scissors. Here it is urgent to observe strict cleanliness, because only thus you avoid infection and festering of the navel. If the remainder of the cord is kept clean, usually in 5 days it falls off completely, without pain to the child. When it falls off, it is necessary to protect the navel with clean yarn for a few days. Very good is clean lard or white petroleum jelly placed on the spot. Wherever the child's navel festers there was uncleanness.

If you want the child to have a clean complexion, do not bathe it immediately after being born, there is plenty of time, until in about 5 hours. It is altogether unnecessary and is harmful to his health. Best is to wipe the phlegm, if there is a lot, with a soft cloth. And even to the breast it is not necessary to put him immediately.

The child should be treated to rest because in his organs started with the movement of lungs an important role, to get rid of the first stool - a blackened residue. That will be removed by the mother's first milk, and that is why both mother and child should have rest, so that the organs, without holding back, can go to work.

A mother should not allow, within a few hours after its coming, that there would be poured into him various medicines or cow's milk. A little screaming will not be harmful to him, because the lungs must expand and this affects the innards like a massage that will then prepare the little citizen for a good appetite. A small amount of lukewarm water with sweet milk, administered with a teaspoon, will be completely adequate for 3-4 hours.

The child's stomach is prepared only for mother's milk and water. For about 9 months, children ought not to be given anything else except milk. If the mothers would conduct themselves according to the laws of nature, children would not die so often and then as adults would not suffer so much with stomach and other organ ailments.

After childbirth the mother should have peace also, because she still needs strength to eject the afterbirth which happens in 15 to 30 minutes after the birth of the child. In a healthy woman this is accomplished without bleeding and pain, and thus the childbirth is ended.

If she feels up to it, she can be cleaned and tended to. If she wants to eat, she can be given some chamomile tea or warm milk, but never greasy food.

In order to help the muscles shrink, it is good to place a cold bandage on the abdomen. During frost and cold weather, the mother must be covered, but leave the window slightly ajar, and light a fire if necessary. There must be no draft. Fresh air is the best medicine for the mother and the newborn.

I should mention that occasionally it *is* necessary to add more food to some children's diet, as the mother sometimes loses her milk too soon, or something similar happens. In this case, use crackers soaked in sweetened water.

It will not be inappropriate to make mention of hard childbirth laboring, which reveals irregularities, which are the result of poor diet or something else which does not agree with the laws of nature. In this case, if the mother suffers severely and cannot give birth, and there is no doctor handy, call the husband. Let him sit opposite her on a chair and hold her feet in his lap, so that the poor woman can have something to lean or push upon. Here one can hand her some warm milk to drink in which a little saffron was boiled.

From my experience, the best achieved was that the mother did not lie in bed, but walked up and down or was led. When the pain was gradually accelerating, she knelt next to a chair on a soft cloth, and with her elbows leaned on the chair, and with her hands pressed from top to bottom on her abdomen.

This way I myself was forced to do in my childbirth hour, as no one else was at home. For this reason, the women on farms should remember to keep everything handy, so that they would have everything when necessary in their moment of need. I experienced much and taught myself to think. I found out that life is not hard, as they say, but people themselves make it hard.

In my mind I fervently wish that this writing will shed light where there was darkness up until now, that it would bring thought where there is none, so that from it would be born new and beautiful comprehension, and from that, peace grow, contentment, and complete happiness, and mainly lead to an increase in morality.

Hygiene and Curative Herbs

Nature everywhere around us sowed an abundance of curative herbs, which should serve man and beast in their bodily afflictions. Mankind, however, to their own loss, do not care about them. Many have I tried, and from experience found out that many are costly and sometimes of little value. Operations could be avoided with a common but powerful extract of a curative herb.

For example, every one of you is familiar with the rose. She announces herself to us in the spring with beautiful rose flowers, which fill the air with a pleasing aroma. Well, then, this flower plucked on the second or third day after blooming, and dried in the shade, can easily be preserved. It has proven to be good when a person has sores on the intestines[73], or during monthly menstruation it is excellent. You take a pinch of the dried flower, pour boiling water over it, and let it stand 10 minutes. If drank while warm, it works well during appendicitis. The extract from these roses even strengthens the heart. If used against ulcers, one should take 2 tablespoons of the potion 3 times.

Another curative herb is garlic - good results are seen against cough. Peel the skin off 2 or 4 buds, chop finely, and place into a cup of boiling milk. Take it once a day for 7 to 8 days. This was tried in the case where a certain person, suffering from unending coughing, was afraid that she was contracting tuberculosis. A short time after using this, the cough disappeared, and she is so healthy that she never even thinks of consumption.

Parsley, dill weed, radishes, and also its root boiled in water, and the extract sipped, gives relief in the curing of kidney stones or sand in the bladder. Rosemary is also one of the very curative herbs, which perhaps grows everywhere. It is picked before blooming and dried. It is cooked the same as tea. It strengthens and refreshes the body. It is best when the extract is mixed with wine.

---

[73] *ulcers*

Rosemary is also good for other ailments. If it happens that a tooth with a cavity hurts, pull off a fresh leaf, chew it up, and hold it on the painful tooth until the pain subsides. Repeat several times.

Whoever suffers from trembling muscles should take rosemary tea 2 times a day at 4 tablespoons, and the malady disappears completely. Boiled in sweet cream and then like oil poured into a crucible, it makes excellent pomade for hair. After every shampoo, if the hair is daubed, thick hair will grow.

Chamomile picked during bloom, and dried in the shade, provides a rich curative tea, which when drank cleans the lungs, liver, kidneys, and mainly spleen, the blood factory, and keeps it clean. It helps during childbirth and helps get rid of the afterbirth. During childbirth it relieves hard working women.

The oil from a juniper tree is another excellent cleaning agent. It removes kidney and bladder stones, and ejects phlegm. This prevents paralysis of muscles and dizziness[74]. They should be taken whole, 3 to 5 seeds a day. Pregnant women must not use them because they strongly affect the fetus. In English they are called "juniper berries."

Dill weed strengthens the stomach and eyesight. It helps expel gases and calms a stifling cough. Because it cleanses it prevents dizziness. For mothers who are breast feeding infants, it helps give abundant milk. It is given in the form of a powder or in dry form, and is scalded and drunk like tea. The green[75] form, boiled and then eaten, works best.

Wormwood, an excellent herb, is picked before blooming and is dried. It is boiled in wine, water, or milk and drank like tea. It cleanses the gall bladder and stomach, and creates rich blood, and aids digestion. It drives away yellow jaundice and edema.

---

[74] *vertigo*
[75] *fresh*

This herb has the good property that when its leaf and stem, boiled and moist, are placed on the ear, it induces sleep and takes out swelling. When the dry leaf is burned, the smoke near the ear strengthens hearing and prevents ringing in the ears.

Lemon is an excellent remedy against cough. The juice is squeezed into a glass, some honey is added, and this makes a syrup and is taken by teaspoonfuls until the cough disappears. For whooping cough in children you take a lemon, six tablespoons of honey, and one-fourth cup water. This is boiled and then is used similarly.

When skin cancer is starting, the first step is to ingest chamomile for cleansing the blood. Then, rub it with sheep's gall or take a clean cloth, let it soak, and with it moisten the cancer. Third, wipe or cut blue lily, pour hot water on it and then wipe the cancer with it. Similarly, cancer can be destroyed by water from rosemary. Next put walnut or hazelnut oil on a tablespoon, hold above a flame, and boil the oil until it is like honey. The warm oil is spread on the cancer at night, and in the morning, and it will perish for certain. It is strange that one method alone will not help, but each one of these in combinations will cure the cancer.

When a rattlesnake or other poisonous snake bites, it is best to take petroleum oil and place the limb into it or if this is not possible wet the bite with the oil until the bile stops leaking out. Another way used in my family is that I chopped some soil, mixed it with water, and placed this around the foot. Horrible pain, which could not be alleviated, quelled; and the swelling, which kept rising up the leg, was restricted by the wet soil. It relieved the pain, which disappeared completely.

Another time it happened that I had blood poison in my toe. The foot was inflamed, the swelling quickly grew, and the pain was becoming unbearable. I could not even move. Crying, I told my husband that in this case, I would not live to see the morning. And he answered that to others I give advice, and to myself I cannot give any help, and he left, returning after a while carrying a pan filled with mud. I placed my foot into it, the pain became weaker, and by morning all was well again.

It is known that slime and mud mixed with vinegar and salt pulls out the heat from swelled veins and muscles, and various poisons from the blood. Sour, settled milk is another good curative way to utilize on any spot where we need to remove poisons. Settled milk is placed on a clean cloth, or the whole limb is submerged in a pan filled with it, and in a few hours relief comes. Even this was tried out in my family, and I give it as a first step, before the doctor arrives.

My little son accidentally stumbled and drove a splinter into his foot. He pulled it out, but the foot hurt although he claimed that he pulled out the whole splinter. When the pain became worse I used mud after mud clabber, but to no avail. Before sending for the doctor, I quickly boiled some water and forced him to put his foot in the water, which was as warm as he could possibly withstand. In a little while, I looked and saw a piece of splinter jutting out. Easily I pulled it out and the blood gushed out. The wound then soon healed.

Cases like these are many, and if parents would remember and always submerge the hurt limb in warm water, squeeze out some blood, and place clean lard on the wound, many children would not have to die. The best salve is a piece of good bacon.

An effective cure is "petrolej"[76]. Not only on snakebites, but to remove in a short time a stifling cough, if on a teaspoon of sugar some petrolej is poured and swallowed.

During a child's diphtheria, this is a proven method. A small clean cloth is taken, and some lard is spread on it or on it are placed pieces of thinly sliced bacon. This is sprinkled with petrolej, placed around the neck, and then a dry warm cloth is wound around the neck. The chest may also be massaged. Then a teaspoon of sugar, and 5 or 6 drops of petrolej are mixed in it and given to the child. Diphtheria in a few hours disappears.

---

[76] *petroleum oil*

When the stomach does not digest, and pains re-echo, it is necessary to take a tablespoon of petrolej, and on an empty stomach swallow it. Do this about twice a week. The other days take a cup of hot water, put in a pinch of salt, and drink it on an empty stomach. In a month's time, every one of you who try it will know the effect of this treatment. The complexion clears, eyes brighten, and the body gains weight. Petrolej cures ulcers in intestines and stomach, and water with salt cleanses the innards.

Furthermore, gall is also a good way to treat a sick stomach. A chick or hen's gall, as soon as removed, should be torn open, and place the contents into a cup of water and drink. It is not delicious, but with its effects it excels over all pills and kalonel.

To get rid of stomach poisonous acids, kitchen soda is taken, only for a while, and it should not be used very often because it causes even the healthy acid to be ejected, and this weakens the stomach.

All the aforementioned curative herbs and instructions of how to use them, people should use with intellect and careful observation of their effect. Individual's natures are not alike, therefore intelligence must be the judge and adviser. Let reason be the director of all your actions - even when you are forced to treat yourself.

For example, how many people suffer with rheumatism or arthritis? And there is nothing better than to soak a cloth in hot salty water, and bind it around the limb. As soon as the cloth is cool, do this again. This is repeated in one or even two hours. If it is necessary to go to work, then after soaking rub the sore limb with lard, apply ammonia and then bandage with a clean, dry cloth. Good also is thick turpentine or birch oil. But if you are aggravated with rheumatism over the body, then it is good (and necessary) to bathe in water as warm as the body can withstand. In the water dissolve salt and Epsom salt. After bathing it is necessary to be careful, so as not to let the ill one catch cold.

Epilogue

This book I offer you so that what is derived from it is for the good of mankind. Every thought herein came from my heart, in the firm conviction that if it is your wish that mankind as soon as possible benefits, you will understand me and continue this work yourselves. Whatever I offer I give with the intention above declared.

I am a wife, mother, and therefore know what it is to suffer. But I remind you that it is not necessary to suffer, and we can avoid much suffering with knowledge. We gain self-knowledge only through profound, deep thinking, reflecting things in nature of which we, humankind, are the most accomplished. Yet, in spite of our faults, we stand closest to God Almighty. We cannot, and must not, expect nature to lead us. It gave us intellect, which we must further refine and supplement. But, alas, that is something that people do not want to do, and then they wonder why we are punished.

Human ignorance is a terrible penalty, where people do not comprehend why they suffer. And may it be said in their favor that they do not know not because they do not want to, but only because they were not granted the opportunity to be acquainted with various truths. No good thing, nor plan, nor finished work fell into a person's lap. Everything to its ripeness needs time and a certain efficiency of execution. People who want to learn are willing to experiment and investigate. Those people deserve a helping hand and honest advice. But the people who are afraid of thought, or the bodily lazy who do not want to think, with this let their fruit fail. Thus they lose their immortality, and at no loss to the world as they are a hindrance to progress.

When during her pregnancies the news was spread that the Russian czarina, wife of Czar Nicholas II, who only bore little girls but wished to have a boy, an idea struck me that I could help her, but I did not know how to reach her. I wrote to several places, even to a certain doctor who worked in Serbia for the Red Cross. He asked me about a lot of things, and then informed me that he believed my understanding was based on truth. He mentioned that it is unknown for what purpose a woman's female organs are divided into two ovaries, right and left, but he alerted me to the fact that most people are indifferent to outward truths, that some revelations they cannot comprehend, and do not want to because they are wanting in experience.

He mentioned that many, after making an error, may roll down the blame on my head that I am either stupid or conceited, or else even a fraud, and therefore he advised me to my advice add financial help - something of substance - that in case of failure I would be protected from litigation. He thought namely that to my advice I should add that it is necessary to drink water, so that in case of failure it could be blamed on faulty use of water.

This advice vexed me, so I ceased using the spoken word to spread my theory about how to produce the desired gender. After a short time that doctor sent me some kind of tablets, advising that I should use them and send them to the Czarina. I thought about it for a while, but it flashed through my mind that perhaps someone is trying to deceive me, or that I might unwittingly deceive someone. Isn't humankind deceived enough already? I decided that I will not deceive anyone nor make a fool of them.

I want to and will tell everyone who wants to know the way that I myself learned and tried to have a child of the desired gender, and if someone's effort does not succeed at first, if he follows the directions it will be successful the next time. Indeed, year after year the people themselves tell me this, and verify the truth of my theory.

That doctor's questionable advice I do not interpret as evil, because in other situations he dealt with me fairly honestly, permitting me to look behind the curtains or facades - where you give the people the truth. Also, it seems to me that after a time this doctor himself wrote to Russia and told the Czarina my theory.

Although today the Czarina is dead, I would give - I don't know what - if I could find out the truth, whether or not my advice was followed, because the Czarina finally did give birth to a son. When through the world spread the news that she was pregnant, I longed to be with her. Even though she was an eminent lady, after all she was just a woman like any other.

How much more a poor woman, a farmer's wife, suffers! Many are surrounded by a crowd of children, and a husband who is maybe indolent or coarse – should they be deceived by false theories? No!

The duty of an honest person is to work toward the goal that our society of people becomes more intelligent, more industrious, and that at the end of his life his conscience would be clear. With this statement I end this book of my experiences, and I send it out into the world to everyone who wants to understand my thoughts, and I wish that my book will contribute to the success of every reader.

May this book also be a sort of journal for the reader. *So for this reason I am including some blank pages so that the reader can make his or her own comments.*

~ THE END ~

Reader's Notes

Reader's Notes

COPY OF AN IMPORTANT LETTER SENT TO THE AUTHOR CONCERNING THE IDENTITY OF "MARIE F.K. CERNY" BY AURELIA JANIK CERNY

November 8, 2005

Dear Maureen:

Received your book and photo yesterday. Great job! I opened the package and started reading and didn't stop until I read the whole book. I would have called you immediately, but I misplaced your telephone number so I had to wait until I had a chance to write. That book is so interesting and I am so glad that you all were able to get this completed, copyright and all.

I am 100% sure that M.F.K. is my husband's grandmother. I reviewed your information on MARIE DUJKA JEZ and I am convinced that they were the authors of this book. My reasons:

MARIE SOMMER CERNY was born Dec. 16, 1858 in House #36 in PCHERY, CZECH REPUBLIC. She married VACLAV (WENCEL) CERNY and had her son JAMES, in 1878. Don't know anything about where she was educated. She was in control of her husband and children (HEARSAY). VACLAV and MARIE must have had some money saved up because when they came to the USA, they settled in NEBRASKA.

After five years of misery, almost freezing and starving, they came by horse and wagon to WALLIS, AUSTIN COUNTY, TEXAS. They were able to purchase over 600 acres of land and soon after their arrival, she became a widow, at age 37. She was able to pay for all that land in a few years. Her youngest child was born about six months after she lost her husband.

VACLAV AND MARIE SOMMER CERNY FAMILY:
JAMES CERNY 1878
ANNA CERNY JUREK 1880
ANTONIE CERNY 1884 infant death
MARY CERNY SCHILLER 1884
ANTONIE CERNY KULHANEK 1886
AGNES CERNY GRIGAR MARTISEK 1890
ROSALIE CERNY GRIGAR 1891
EMILY CERNY KLECKA 1893
FRANK CERNY 1895

She farmed with her children and after they all left home to begin their own families, she retired and moved to town. Her oldest son JAMES and his wife and family owned a store in town. She lived in a small home on GRESHAM STREET. The house was still there a couple of years ago; the ladies at city hall informed me that the home was demolished some time ago. She lived in this home from 1920 to 1923. I have a copy of her death record from GUARDIAN ANGEL CATHOLIC CHURCH. She is buried at KRASNA next to her husband. VACLAV CERNY was one of the first settlers of KRASNA and was one of the first to be buried there in 1894. That was the only cemetery around this region. I have copies of letters from Marie's sister from CZECH REPUBLIC addressed to her in WALLIS, TEXAS.

Maureen, I went to Wallis today and found the cute home that Marie Jez lived in. Where was her farm located? *[Author's note: The farm is located near the present Brazos High School location in Wallis, Texas.]* Their homes were across the tracks from each other. I am sure they visited on a regular basis.

As I read this book, I was amazed to read things my mother-in-law, LOUISE DUSEK CERNY would tell me about her mother-in-law, MARIE SOMMER CERNY. I was newly married to JEROME CERNY and we farmed for a while with JEROME'S parents.

When we picked cotton, LOUISE would tell me all these stories about her mother-in-law. The same advice about home remedies, wars, etc. The two didn't get along very well so her stories were all one-sided.

The reason she used "M.F.K. Cerny" [*Author's note: instead of MARIE CERNY, or MARIE SOMMER CERNY, or M.S. CERNY*], I can only guess. By the time MARIE CERNY died, there were two other little girls in WALLIS, TEXAS, named MARIE CERNY.

One was born Oct. 18, 1906, to JAMES and LOUISE VIACLOVSKY CERNY. Another baby was born Aug. 15, 1921, to FRANK and LOUISE CERNY. Am sure that M.F.K. CERNY decided that by now she needed her own identification, especially if she was involved in writing a book.

Perhaps: M. = MARIE, F. = FRANTISEK (her father's name), K. = KRASKA as she came from the KRASNA settlement. [*Author's note: Perhaps MARIE CERNY chose to use the middle initials, "F.K.", because for some reason she preferred to disguise her identity.*]

COMPARISON OF THE TWO LADIES:

MARIE JEZ:	MARIE CERNY:
b. 1859	b. 1858
d. 1930, age 71	d. 1923, age 65
widowed at age 52	widowed at age 37
moved from farm to town, 1921	moved from farm to town, 1920

They were both widows at a young age. They both had a bunch of kids. They worked hard on their farms. Both were very successful in life. Truly smart women.

Maureen, I want to purchase more books from you to donate to the WALLIS LIBRARY and one to TCHCC and one to CHS of Texas, CHS of Fort Bend County.

Let me know if you will add any of this or if your book is final. Again, GREAT JOB! You didn't tell me you had a DR. DEGREE.

GOD'S BLESSINGS!

AURELIA JANIK CERNY

P.S. I used to go by the name of MARIE CERNY. I now have a daughter-in-law named that, so I went back to my given name. Also, if you don't mind, give me your telephone # again and when is a good time to chat.

AUTHOR'S NOTE: In the year 2000, Aurelia Janik Cerny published an informative, comprehensive, and entertaining book entitled CERNY SOMER ROOTS IN CZECH REPUBLIC, which contains important history of interest to anyone interested in Czech heritage. Aurelia dedicated her work to the memory of WENCEL and MARIE SOMMER[77] CERNY. To order a copy, please contact Aurelia by mail at 506 Alcorn, Sugar Land, Texas, 77478.

---

[77] *In her book, Aurelia noted that Marie's maiden name ("Sommer") was spelled two ways. On the tombstone it is spelled "Somer."*

ABOUT THE AUTHOR

Maureen Polasek Viaclovsky

Maureen Viaclovsky is married to the love of her life, Sylvester (Syl) Alois Viaclovsky. They have two sons who enrich their lives immeasurably: Sylvester (Syl) Charles Viaclovsky, and Jeffrey (Jeff) Alan Viaclovsky. Syl Charles is presently single and has three children: Sylvester Allen Viaclovsky, Anna Rosalee Viaclovsky, and Charles Jeffery Viaclovsky. Jeffrey Alan is married to Tomoko (Yoshinaga) Viaclovsky.

Maureen's most rewarding roles in life have been as a wife, mother, and grandparent. In addition, she has always valued strong family ties with extended family. Maureen joins her great – grandmother (Marie Jez), her mother (Bessie Ann Jez Polasek), father (Charles Polasek), and other relatives who share her lifelong love of reading, quest for knowledge, and enjoyment of friends and family.

These influences led Maureen to additional occupations such as regular education teacher, special education teacher, and educational diagnostician. She attained a doctorate degree in educational psychology in 1990. "Dr. V" (a fond nickname bestowed on her by co-workers) is a dedicated psychologist currently working part time in a school district near her home.

Maureen is grateful to have had a role in continuing the work her mother (Bessie Ann Jez Polasek) began when she devoted many hours, days and years to translating Marie Jez's book. She is equally grateful for the opportunity to share this "labor of love" family heritage work with others.

Ordering Information

Additional copies of this publication for self or for gifts to others (e.g., to children and other family descendants), may be ordered from www.createspace.com/3480560 or Amazon.com. Search on Amazon.com and other websites, such as Google.com, for the author's name or the book title: *My Great-Grandmother's Lost, Banned, Burned Book: A Miraculous Find.*

Contact the author if you are unable to locate copies of this book or if you would like to offer additional information:

E-mail: maureen.viaclovsky@gmail.com

Or write to: Maureen Viaclovsky
2106 Airline Drive
Friendswood, Texas 77456

*For genealogy buffs, surnames mentioned in this book include the following: **Adamik, Alvarez, Barta, Beca, Becica, Bercak, Bergeron, Bolf, Boone, Brenk, Brod, Caves, Cerny (spelled "Cerna" in Czech), Cervenka, Chalupa, Cho, Cico, Connelly, Cook, Dujka, Dusek, Duyka, Ernstes, Faktor, Foltyn, Flowers, Gardner, Grigar, Hadjik, Haedge, Harrison, Hereford, Hubenak, Janik, Jez, Jones, Jurek, Kapavik, Kay, Klecka, Korenek, Kostalnik, Krchnak, Krecicek, Kubricht, Kulcak, Kulhanek, Lastovica, Listak, Lubojacky, Macik, Malek, Martisek, Mican, Mieth, Mikes, Mize, Mlcak, Nezhoda, Orsak, Pavlicek, Pavlovsky, Peacock, Pechal, Peters, Polasek, Provazek, Pyka, Raska, Reuss, Rickaway, Rousseau, Saha, Schauerte, Schiller, Schneider, Sebestiana, Smith, Sodolak, Somer, Sommer, Sowa, Surovcek, Svoboda, Thomas, Toman, Tomanec, Tuma, Tyl, Vaclavic, Vaclavick, Vargus, Viaclovsky, Vrazel, Ward, Whiclep, Yoshinaga.***

46442830R00077

Made in the USA
Lexington, KY
03 November 2015